This Day, That Hi
Shocking, Strange, a
Stories from the Past

Introduction:

History doesn't just live in textbooks, documentaries, or the dusty corners of libraries. It breathes in every single day. Each date on your calendar is a door and if you open it, you'll find stories of daring kings, failed invasions, scientific breakthroughs, political chaos, revolutions, assassinations, and bizarre moments that are almost too strange to be true.

This book brings you one historical event for every day of the year. Not just names and dates but real stories. The kind of stories that shaped the world we live in, stunned the people who lived through them, or whispered quietly in the background while the world kept turning. From blood-soaked battlefields to candle lit invention rooms, you're about to time-travel through the centuries, one day at a time.

With each day, there will be a few paragraphs telling the tale that are: clear, gripping, and packed with detail. Not too much to bore you, but not too little to leave you guessing. Just the right amount to teach you something new without turning it into a lecture. You can read this book one day at a time, letting history unfold as the calendar turns, or you can race through it at your own pace, uncovering back-to-back moments that shook the world. Some stories you'll know, others will catch you off guard but every single one really happened and helped shape the world we live in.

So, grab a seat (or a time machine) and get ready to discover what made *this day... that history*.

January 1st

1959 – Fidel Castro Seizes Power in Cuba

On New Year's Day 1959, the government of Cuban dictator Fulgencio Batista collapsed, and Fidel Castro officially took control. After years of guerrilla warfare in the mountains, Castro's revolutionary forces marched triumphantly into Havana, bringing an end to decades of U.S.-backed dictatorship and beginning a new era in Cuban history.

Batista had fled the country in the early hours of the morning, taking with him millions in stolen funds and leaving behind a regime on the brink of implosion. Castro, who had led the 26th of July Movement, promised to bring justice, land reform, and independence to the Cuban people. Many initially welcomed his leadership, hoping for democratic change.

However, what followed was a complete transformation of the island's political and economic systems. Castro nationalized industries aligned Cuba with the Soviet Union and declared socialism as the state's guiding principle. This led to decades of tension with the United States, including the infamous Bay of Pigs invasion and the Cuban Missile Crisis of 1962.

Castro's rise wasn't just the start of a new government but it was the spark that turned Cuba into a Cold War flashpoint and cemented its place on the global stage for the next half-century.

January 2nd

1492 – The Moors Surrender Granada, Ending the Reconquista

On this day, the last Muslim stronghold in Spain fell. After nearly 800 years of Islamic rule in parts of the Iberian Peninsula, the Emirate of Granada surrendered to the Catholic Monarchs, Ferdinand II of Aragon and Isabella I of Castile.

The surrender marked the end of the Reconquista, a long series of military campaigns by Christian kingdoms to reclaim territory from Muslim rule. Granada had been the final Muslim-controlled city since the fall of other regions in the 13th century. The peaceful surrender was negotiated under relatively generous terms for the Muslim population, promising religious freedom and protection. However, within a few years, these terms were broken, leading to forced conversions, persecution, and the eventual expulsion of Muslims and Jews from Spain.

The victory was deeply symbolic for Christian Europe and helped to solidify Spain's emerging identity as a united Catholic kingdom. It also freed up resources for the monarchs to fund new ventures, including a voyage by a certain Genoese navigator later that same year.

January 3rd

1920 – The Boston Red Sox agree to Sell Babe Ruth to the New York Yankees

On this day, the Boston Red Sox made one of the most infamous deals in sports history. Owner Harry Frazee made the deal to sell 25-year-old slugger Babe Ruth to the New York Yankees for $125,000 in cash and a $350,000 loan. At the time, Ruth was already a rising star, having led the league in home runs and brought the Red Sox three World Series titles. It was officially announced on the 5th of Jan.

The real reason for the sale was financial. Frazee was heavily in debt and wanted to fund a Broadway musical. Ruth, meanwhile, had been clashing with management and demanding a raise. Frazee saw an opportunity to cash in but few could have imagined the long-term fallout.

After Ruth's departure, the Red Sox entered a decades-long championship drought, failing to win a World Series for 86 years. The Yankees, on the other hand, became the most dominant franchise in baseball. Fans soon began talking about a curse which was the "Curse of the Bambino" blaming Ruth's sale for the team's terrible luck. Whether you believe in curses or not, the numbers tell the story: from 1920 onward, the Yankees thrived, and Boston suffered.

January 4th
1847 – Samuel Colt sells his first revolver pistol to the United States government

In 1847, inventor Samuel Colt made history when he secured his first major contract with the United States government. On this day, he sold his Colt revolver to the U.S. Army, marking the beginning of a firearms revolution. The deal came at a time when the military was seeking more efficient, reliable weapons for its soldiers, particularly as the Mexican-American War loomed. Colt's design which was a six-shooter revolver capable of firing multiple rounds without reloading was groundbreaking.

The model he sold, known as the Colt Walker, was a collaboration between Colt and Texas Ranger Captain Samuel Walker, who needed a powerful sidearm for use on the battlefield. The resulting weapon was enormous by today's standards, weighing over four pounds, but it packed unmatched firepower for its time. The government ordered 1,000 units, manufactured by Eli Whitney Jr. (son of the cotton gin inventor), helping Colt revive his struggling business.

This sale not only saved Colt from financial ruin but also launched one of the most iconic names in firearms history. The Colt revolver would go on to become a symbol of the American frontier and a staple of both military and civilian arsenals for decades to come.

January 5th
1971 – The body of former boxing champion Sonny Liston is found dead in his Las Vegas home

On this day in 1971, the lifeless body of former world heavyweight boxing champion Charles "Sonny" Liston was discovered by his wife Geraldine at their Las Vegas home. He had been dead for several days , possibly as many as six and the cause of death has remained a source of controversy ever since. Officially, the coroner ruled it as heart failure, with traces of heroin found in his system. But many, including those close to him, doubted the story.

Liston's death raised immediate suspicion. There were no needle marks on his body, and those who knew him claimed he had a deep fear of needles. Rumours of foul play quickly spread, especially given his known connections to organized crime. Some speculated that he may have been silenced to prevent him from speaking out or crossing the wrong people. Others believed his lifestyle which was marked by substance use and turbulent relationships had finally caught up with him.

Liston's boxing legacy was equally complicated. Once the most feared man in the ring, he lost his title to a young Muhammad Ali in a historic upset. Though overshadowed by scandal and mystery, Liston remains one of boxing's most powerful and enigmatic figures. His death, like his life, left more questions than answers.

January 6th

1809 – Allied Forces Begin the Invasion of Cayenne – Napoleonic wars

On this day, British, Portuguese, and Brazilian colonial troops launched an amphibious assault on Cayenne, the capital of French Guiana. The operation was part of the wider Napoleonic Wars and marked one of the few military campaigns fought in South America during that period.

The French colony had long served as a strategic base in the region. With France heavily engaged in Europe, its overseas territories were vulnerable. Britain, eager to weaken Napoleon's global reach, worked with Portugal and its Brazilian colony to mount the operation. The allied force was small, but well-organized and included local soldiers from Brazil.

Landing just outside the city, the attackers quickly overwhelmed the French defenders. After a brief but intense engagement, Cayenne surrendered by early January 1809. The victory handed control of the colony to the Portuguese, who administered it until the end of the Napoleonic Wars in 1814.

Though often overlooked, the invasion of Cayenne was a rare example of colonial cooperation and a reminder that the Napoleonic Wars extended far beyond European borders.

January 7th

1610 – Galileo Galilei Discovers Jupiter's Moons

On the night of January 7th, 1610, Italian astronomer Galileo Galilei turned his homemade telescope toward Jupiter and saw something extraordinary - three small "stars" near the planet. Within days, he spotted a fourth. These weren't stars at all, but moons orbiting Jupiter: Io, Europa, Ganymede, and Callisto.

The discovery shook the foundations of astronomy. Until then, the prevailing belief was that all heavenly bodies revolved around the Earth. Galileo's observations offered direct evidence that not everything in the universe orbited our planet. It supported the Copernican model, which placed the Sun and not the Earth at the centre of the solar system.

Galileo published his findings in *Sidereus Nuncius* just two months later. The book caused a sensation and also sparked outrage from religious authorities. He would later face trial for heresy.

Today, the four moons he discovered are known as the Galilean satellites. They remain a focus of scientific interest, especially Europa, which may harbour a subsurface ocean. But it all began with a telescope, a clear night, and a man who dared to look closer.

January 8th

1815 – The Battle of New Orleans Ends the War of 1812 (Sort Of)

On January 8th, 1815, American troops under General Andrew Jackson delivered a decisive victory against British forces at the Battle of New Orleans. Over 2,000 British soldiers were killed, wounded, or captured, while American casualties were fewer than 100. It was one of the most lopsided and celebrated victories in U.S. military history.

But there was a twist: the war was technically already over. The Treaty of Ghent had been signed in Europe on December 24th, 1814, ending the War of 1812. News of the treaty hadn't reached America yet, so the battle went ahead as planned.

Jackson's victory turned him into a national hero and eventually propelled him to the presidency. For many Americans, the battle symbolized a second war for independence — a moment when the young republic stood up to the might of the British Empire and won.

Despite its odd timing, the Battle of New Orleans had a lasting impact. It boosted national pride, weakened Native American resistance in the Southeast, and cemented Jackson's place in U.S. history.

January 9th

1768 – Philip Astley Stages the First Modern Circus in London

In a muddy field near Westminster Bridge, Philip Astley, a former cavalryman, set up a circular performance ring and staged what would become the blueprint for the modern circus. The date was January 9th, 1768, and the event combined trick horse riding with acrobatics, clowning, and feats of strength.

Astley had noticed that performing in a circle allowed riders to use centrifugal force to maintain balance. He added musicians and comic acts to keep audiences entertained between horse tricks. It was this blend of showmanship and skill that turned a niche performance into a public sensation.

The concept quickly spread across Europe. Within decades, circuses popped up in cities from Paris to St. Petersburg. Later innovations brought in animals, tightrope walkers, and traveling tents, but the circular ring and variety format remained at the heart of the show.

Astley didn't invent every part of the circus, but he brought it all together. His idea transformed street entertainment into a full-fledged cultural phenomenon that would delight audiences for generations.

January 10th

49 BC – Julius Caesar Crosses the Rubicon, Igniting Civil War

On this fateful day, Julius Caesar led his legion across the Rubicon River in northern Italy, a direct violation of Roman law that forbade any general from bringing an army into the heart of the Republic. As his soldiers marched forward, Caesar is said to have declared, "Alea iacta est" – the die is cast.

The move was a clear act of rebellion against the Roman Senate. Tensions had been building for years between Caesar and the conservative faction led by Pompey and the Senate elite. By crossing the Rubicon, Caesar made it clear he would not submit to orders demanding his disbandment and prosecution. The Republic, already politically fragile, plunged into civil war.

Caesar's gamble paid off. Within three years, he had defeated Pompey, seized control of Rome, and declared himself dictator for life. Though his rule was cut short by assassination in 44 BC, the moment at the Rubicon marked the beginning of the end for the Roman Republic and the rise of imperial rule.

The phrase "crossing the Rubicon" has since become shorthand for passing a point of no return — and Caesar's decision remains one of the most defining in world history.

January 11th

1908 – Grand Canyon Declared a National Monument by Theodore Roosevelt

On January 11th, 1908, U.S. President Theodore Roosevelt used his authority under the Antiquities Act to declare the Grand Canyon a national monument. This bold move was aimed at protecting one of America's greatest natural wonders from exploitation and development.

Roosevelt had visited the canyon years earlier and was struck by its vast beauty. "Leave it as it is," he had famously said. "You cannot improve on it." At the time, mining interests were keen to extract copper and other resources from the region, and there was growing concern that the landscape would be ruined without federal protection.

Declaring it a monument was the first major step in preserving the area. It wouldn't become a full national park until 1919, but Roosevelt's designation stopped industrial development in its tracks.

Today, the Grand Canyon draws millions of visitors every year. Roosevelt's decision helped spark a national conservation movement and remains one of the earliest and most powerful examples of U.S. environmental policy in action.

January 12th

1879 – British Forces Invade Zululand, Starting the Anglo-Zulu War

The Anglo-Zulu War began on January 12th, 1879, when British troops crossed the Buffalo River into Zululand, present-day South Africa. The invasion was ordered by Lord Chelmsford after the Zulu king, Cetshwayo, refused to disband his army and submit to British control.

The British had issued an ultimatum in December 1878, knowing it would be impossible for the Zulus to accept. The real aim was to provoke conflict and bring the powerful Zulu Kingdom under colonial rule. The invasion force was well-equipped but underestimated its opponent.

Just over a week later, the British suffered a catastrophic defeat at the Battle of Isandlwana, where thousands of imperial troops were killed by Zulu warriors. Though the British eventually regrouped and won the war by July, the early stages exposed the arrogance and miscalculations of imperial leadership.

The war destroyed the independence of the Zulu Kingdom and expanded British influence in southern Africa. It also sparked debates back in Britain about the ethics and cost of imperial conquest.

January 13th

1898 – Émile Zola Publishes *J'Accuse...!* in Defense of Alfred Dreyfus

On January 13th, 1898, French author Émile Zola published an open letter in the newspaper *L'Aurore*, titled *J'Accuse...!* The letter, addressed to the French President, was a blistering indictment of the government's handling of the Dreyfus Affair, a political scandal that had gripped the country.

Captain Alfred Dreyfus, a Jewish officer in the French army, had been wrongly convicted of treason in 1894. Evidence later emerged that another officer was guilty, but the military covered it up. Zola's letter accused top officials of antisemitism, corruption, and a conspiracy to protect their own.

The fallout was immediate. Zola was charged with libel and fled the country, but his letter electrified public opinion. It helped launch the Dreyfusard movement, which demanded justice and accountability. Eventually, Dreyfus was exonerated and reinstated in the army.

J'Accuse...! remains one of the most powerful examples of speaking truth to power. It turned a novelist into a national conscience and forced France to reckon with the dark undercurrents of prejudice and injustice in its institutions.

January 14th

1954 – Marilyn Monroe Marries Baseball Legend Joe DiMaggio

On January 14th, 1954, Hollywood's brightest star and America's baseball hero tied the knot. Marilyn Monroe and Joe DiMaggio were married in a small civil ceremony at San Francisco's City Hall, surrounded by a crowd of photographers and fans eager for a glimpse of the couple.

Their romance had captivated the country. Monroe was at the height of her fame, a symbol of glamour and vulnerability, while DiMaggio had retired the year before as one of baseball's all-time greats. But behind the scenes, the relationship was already strained.

DiMaggio reportedly struggled with Monroe's image as a sex symbol and disliked her growing independence. Just nine months after the wedding, the couple divorced, citing irreconcilable differences. Despite the short marriage, DiMaggio remained devoted to Monroe for the rest of his life. He famously sent roses to her grave every week for two decades after her death.

The marriage of Monroe and DiMaggio was brief but iconic, capturing a unique moment in American pop culture where fame, beauty, and tragedy collided.

January 15th

2009 – Miracle on the Hudson: US Airways Flight 1549 Lands Safely in River

Just after takeoff from New York's LaGuardia Airport on January 15th, 2009, US Airways Flight 1549 struck a flock of geese. Both engines failed. With no power and little time, Captain Chesley "Sully" Sullenberger made the decision to ditch the Airbus A320 into the Hudson River.

The landing was flawless. All 155 people on board survived. Passengers stood on the wings as ferry boats and rescue crews arrived within minutes. The image of the half-submerged plane floating in icy waters quickly became a symbol of calm under pressure.

The event was nicknamed the "Miracle on the Hudson," but it was no miracle. It was the result of expert training, steady nerves, and decisive action. Sullenberger became a national hero overnight, though he insisted it was a team effort involving the entire flight crew.

The incident led to changes in pilot training and a renewed appreciation for the professionalism of airline crews. In a time of economic uncertainty and political tension, it was a rare story of everything going right.

January 16th

1920 – Prohibition Begins in the United States

At midnight on January 16th, 1920, the 18th Amendment to the U.S. Constitution came into effect, ushering in the era of Prohibition. The manufacture, sale, and transportation of alcohol were now banned across the country.

Driven by a coalition of religious reformers, temperance advocates, and moral crusaders, Prohibition aimed to eliminate the social problems caused by alcohol abuse. However, rather than creating a more virtuous society, it gave rise to bootlegging, speakeasies, and organized crime.

Figures like Al Capone thrived, building empires on the illegal alcohol trade. Law enforcement struggled to keep up, and public respect for the law declined. Ironically, alcohol consumption may have even increased in some areas, as Americans found creative ways to bypass restrictions.

After thirteen turbulent years, Prohibition was repealed in 1933 with the 21st Amendment. Its legacy is a cautionary tale about the limits of legislation in shaping personal behaviour, and a vivid example of how good intentions can backfire when public support is lacking.

January 17th

1945 – Soviet Forces Enter Warsaw, Ending German Occupation

On January 17th, 1945, Soviet troops of the Red Army entered the shattered Polish capital of Warsaw, ending over five years of brutal Nazi occupation. The city, once home to 1.3 million people, lay in ruins.

Warsaw had endured some of the harshest conditions of World War II. After resisting the German invasion in 1939, it became a centre of resistance. The 1944 Warsaw Uprising, led by the Polish Home Army, was crushed after two months of bitter street fighting. In retaliation, the Germans destroyed much of the city and massacred tens of thousands.

When the Soviets finally advanced, they found a ghost town. Most of the population was dead or displaced. Although their arrival brought relief from Nazi rule, it also marked the beginning of a new chapter under Soviet control. Poland would remain behind the Iron Curtain for the next four decades.

The liberation of Warsaw remains a sombre turning point — a victory overshadowed by devastation and political betrayal.

January 18th

1778 – Captain James Cook Becomes the First European to Discover Hawaii

British explorer Captain James Cook sighted the Hawaiian Islands on January 18th, 1778, during his third and final voyage across the Pacific. He named them the "Sandwich Islands" after the Earl of Sandwich, First Lord of the Admiralty.

Cook and his crew were greeted with hospitality by the native islanders. The islands were a thriving society with complex traditions and political systems. At first, the encounter was peaceful and marked by mutual curiosity. Cook was impressed by the navigational skills of the Hawaiians and the richness of their culture.

However, later visits would sour. Just over a year after his discovery, Cook was killed in a confrontation on the Big Island following a dispute over a stolen boat. His death was a tragic end to one of the most ambitious voyages in maritime history.

Cook's landing opened Hawaii to the wider world. While it marked the beginning of global interest in the islands, it also set in motion a series of events that would ultimately lead to colonization, disease outbreaks, and cultural loss for native Hawaiians.

January 19th

1809 – Edgar Allan Poe Is Born in Boston, Massachusetts

One of the most influential writers in American literature, Edgar Allan Poe was born on January 19th, 1809. Known for his haunting poems and chilling short stories, Poe pioneered the genres of Gothic fiction, psychological horror, and the detective story.

Orphaned by age three, Poe lived a troubled life marked by poverty, addiction, and heartbreak. Despite these hardships, he produced a remarkable body of work. Poems like "The Raven" and stories such as "The Tell-Tale Heart" and "The Fall of the House of Usher" earned him lasting fame.

In 1841, Poe published "The Murders in the Rue Morgue," widely considered the first modern detective story. His ability to explore the darker corners of the human mind set him apart from his contemporaries and earned him the title "Master of the Macabre."

Poe died mysteriously in 1849 at the age of 40. Though his life was brief, his impact on literature was immense. He continues to inspire writers, filmmakers, and readers who find beauty in the eerie and the tragic.

January 20th

1981 – Ronald Reagan Sworn in as President as U.S. Hostages Are Freed

On January 20th, 1981, Ronald Reagan was inaugurated as the 40th President of the United States. Just minutes later, 52 American hostages held in Iran for 444 days were released, ending one of the most humiliating diplomatic crises in U.S. history.

The Iran Hostage Crisis had begun in November 1979, when radical students stormed the U.S. Embassy in Tehran. The hostages became symbols of national frustration during Jimmy Carter's presidency, and his failure to secure their release likely cost him re-election.

The timing of their release which was immediately after Reagan took office was no coincidence. It was seen by many as a final snub to Carter and a signal of a new, tougher American stance. Though negotiations had been underway for months, Reagan's team capitalized on the dramatic moment.

Reagan's inauguration and the end of the hostage crisis marked a turning point in American politics. The "Reagan Era" had begun, with a bold promise of strength at home and abroad.

January 21st

1793 – King Louis XVI Executed by Guillotine in Revolutionary France

On a cold morning in Paris, January 21st, 1793, King Louis XVI was executed in front of a massive crowd. Convicted of treason during the French Revolution, the former monarch was guillotined in the Place de la Révolution, ending centuries of absolute monarchy in France.

Louis had been a weak and indecisive ruler during a time of extreme political and economic turmoil. As revolutionary fervour swept the nation, he was caught trying to flee the country and later put on trial by the new Republic.

The execution shocked Europe. Monarchies across the continent condemned the act, fearing similar uprisings. In France, it deepened the divide between revolutionaries and royalists, fuelling the violence of the Reign of Terror.

Though seen by many as justice, Louis's death also marked the beginning of more radical and bloody phases of the revolution. It remains one of the most defining and controversial moments in European history.

January 22nd

1901 – Queen Victoria Dies After 63 Years on the Throne

Queen Victoria, the longest-reigning monarch in British history at the time, died on January 22nd, 1901, at the age of 81. Her passing marked the end of the Victorian era and the beginning of a new century for the British Empire.

Victoria came to the throne in 1837 and oversaw a period of immense change. The British Empire expanded to its height, industrialization transformed daily life, and scientific breakthroughs redefined the modern world. Her reign was also marked by deep personal tragedy, including the death of her beloved husband Prince Albert in 1861.

Mourning Albert for the rest of her life, Victoria wore black until her death and retreated from public life for many years. Despite this, she became a powerful symbol of continuity and imperial pride.

Her funeral was attended by leaders from across the globe, and her death signalled the close of a chapter. The Edwardian age that followed would be briefer, more uncertain, and increasingly shaped by modern forces beyond the control of monarchs.

January 23rd

1556 – Deadliest Earthquake in Recorded History Strikes Shaanxi, China

On January 23rd, 1556, a devastating earthquake struck the Chinese province of Shaanxi, killing an estimated 830,000 people. It remains the deadliest earthquake ever recorded.

The quake, estimated to be around magnitude 8.0, flattened entire villages and cities. Many people in the region lived in loess caves and soft, porous hillsides that collapsed instantly when the earth shook. Landslides and fires followed, worsening the destruction.

The region's dense population and poor construction methods contributed to the catastrophic death toll. Contemporary accounts described widespread panic, with survivors struggling to find food, shelter, and clean water.

In the aftermath, the Ming Dynasty implemented some reforms in building practices, but the full scale of the disaster could never truly be undone. Even today, historians and seismologists study the 1556 quake for insights into tectonic activity and disaster preparedness.

The Shaanxi earthquake stands as a tragic reminder of nature's power and the human cost of vulnerability in the face of disaster.

January 24th

1965 – Winston Churchill Dies at the Age of 90

On January 24th, 1965, Sir Winston Churchill passed away in London. One of Britain's greatest statesmen, Churchill led the nation through its darkest hour during World War II and became a global symbol of resistance and defiance.

Born in 1874, Churchill had a long and often controversial political career. He served in numerous government roles before becoming Prime Minister in 1940, just as Nazi Germany threatened to conquer Europe. His rousing speeches, including "We shall fight on the beaches," helped rally British morale.

Churchill's leadership during the war earned him global acclaim, but his postwar years were more mixed. He lost the 1945 election, returned to power in 1951, then retired for good in 1955. He was awarded the Nobel Prize in Literature in 1953 and was made an honorary U.S. citizen in 1963.

His state funeral was attended by world leaders and watched by millions. Churchill's legacy endures as a defender of freedom, a master of language, and a titan of history.

January 25th

1971 – Idi Amin Seizes Power in Uganda After Military Coup

On this day, General Idi Amin took control of Uganda in a swift and unexpected military coup, ousting President Milton Obote while he was away on a foreign trip. Amin, who had risen through the ranks of the British colonial army, declared himself president and promised a return to stability. What followed instead was one of the most brutal regimes in African history.

Amin ruled Uganda with an iron fist for eight years. During his dictatorship, an estimated 300,000 people were killed. He targeted political opponents, ethnic groups, intellectuals, and anyone who threatened his power. His erratic behavior and violent purges earned him global notoriety.

He also expelled Uganda's Asian minority in 1972, many of whom were vital to the country's economy. This led to economic collapse and international condemnation. Eventually, in 1979, Amin's forces were defeated by a coalition of Ugandan exiles and the Tanzanian army. He fled into exile, never facing justice for his crimes.

His rule left Uganda deeply scarred and stands as a grim warning about the dangers of unchecked military power and authoritarian rule.

January 26th

1788 – First Fleet Arrives in Australia and Establishes British Penal Colony

On January 26th, 1788, the First Fleet of British ships landed at Port Jackson, in what is now Sydney, Australia. Led by Captain Arthur Phillip, the fleet carried over 1,000 people, including convicts, soldiers, and officials. This marked the founding of the first European settlement on the Australian continent.

Britain had begun transporting convicts to relieve overcrowded prisons at home. After losing its American colonies, it sought a new place for penal relocation. The British government chose Botany Bay, but upon arrival found it unsuitable, prompting a move to the more sheltered Port Jackson.

For Indigenous Australians, the arrival signalled the beginning of profound disruption. Colonisation brought disease, displacement, and violence to Aboriginal communities, who had lived on the land for over 60,000 years.

Today, January 26th is celebrated as Australia Day, but it is also observed as a day of mourning and protest by many Indigenous people. The date remains deeply controversial, symbolising both the birth of modern Australia and the start of a painful colonial legacy.

January 27th

1945 – Soviet Troops Liberate Auschwitz Concentration Camp

On January 27th, 1945, soldiers of the Soviet Red Army entered the Auschwitz concentration camp in Nazi-occupied Poland and liberated over 7,000 prisoners. What they found shocked even the most hardened veterans of war: emaciated survivors, piles of corpses, and the infrastructure of mass extermination.

Auschwitz was the largest and most notorious of all Nazi death camps. Over 1.1 million people, mostly Jews, were murdered there between 1940 and 1945. Victims were gassed, shot, starved, and subjected to inhumane medical experiments.

The liberation of Auschwitz exposed the full horror of the Holocaust to the world. Survivors bore the physical and emotional scars for life. The camp has since become a symbol of genocide, evil, and the dangers of unchecked hatred and totalitarianism.

January 27th is now commemorated as International Holocaust Remembrance Day. It stands as a day to honour the victims, remember the atrocities, and ensure that such a tragedy never happens again.

January 28th

1986 – Space Shuttle Challenger Disintegrates After Launch, Killing All Seven Crew

On the morning of January 28th, 1986, millions watched in horror as NASA's Space Shuttle Challenger broke apart just 73 seconds after liftoff. The disaster killed all seven astronauts on board, including Christa McAuliffe, who was to be the first civilian teacher in space.

The launch had been delayed several times due to weather and technical issues. Despite unusually cold temperatures that morning, NASA proceeded. Unknown to the public at the time, engineers had expressed concerns about the failure of rubber O-rings in the solid rocket boosters due to the cold.

Their fears were tragically realised. A faulty seal allowed hot gases to escape and destroy part of the shuttle's structure. The vehicle disintegrated high in the sky, leaving a stunned nation in grief.

The Challenger disaster led to a full suspension of NASA's shuttle program and a major investigation. It exposed deep flaws in NASA's decision-making culture and brought sweeping changes to spaceflight safety procedures. The memory of the crew lives on in schools, scholarships, and memorials across the world.

January 29th

1845 – Edgar Allan Poe's "The Raven" Is First Published

On January 29th, 1845, "The Raven," Edgar Allan Poe's most famous poem, was published in the New York Evening Mirror. The haunting verse, with its musical rhythm and themes of grief and madness, made Poe an overnight sensation and cemented his place in American literary history.

The poem tells the story of a mourning man visited by a mysterious raven that only speaks one word: "Nevermore." As the narrator descends into despair, the raven becomes a symbol of the permanence of death and the loss of his beloved Lenore.

"The Raven" captivated readers with its eerie mood and masterful structure. Poe's use of internal rhyme, alliteration, and trochaic octameter created a hypnotic and unforgettable reading experience.

Though Poe earned only a modest sum for the poem, its impact was enormous. It remains a staple of English literature and has inspired countless interpretations, adaptations, and references in popular culture. "The Raven" endures as a masterpiece of Gothic poetry and a testament to Poe's genius.

January 30th

1948 – Mahatma Gandhi Assassinated in New Delhi

On January 30th, 1948, Mohandas Karamchand Gandhi, the spiritual leader of India's independence movement, was assassinated in New Delhi by Hindu nationalist Nathuram Godse. Gandhi's death sent shockwaves across the world and plunged India into mourning.

Gandhi had devoted his life to non-violent resistance and social reform. Through hunger strikes, protests, and peaceful defiance, he led India's struggle against British rule, culminating in independence in 1947. He was revered not just in India, but around the world as a symbol of peace and human dignity.

However, Gandhi's calls for unity between Hindus and Muslims angered extremists who saw him as too conciliatory. Godse believed Gandhi's policies had weakened Hindu India and took matters into his own hands.

Gandhi was shot three times at close range as he walked to a prayer meeting. His last words were reportedly "Hey Ram." His death was a profound loss to the world. Today, his birthday is observed as the International Day of Non-Violence.

January 31st

1606 – Guy Fawkes Executed for Gunpowder Plot Against English Parliament

On January 31st, 1606, Guy Fawkes was hanged, drawn, and quartered in London for his role in the failed Gunpowder Plot of 1605. The plot aimed to blow up King James I and the House of Lords during the State Opening of Parliament, in a bold attempt to restore Catholic rule in England.

Fawkes had been discovered guarding barrels of gunpowder beneath the House of Lords in the early hours of November 5th. His arrest led to the capture of his co-conspirators, who were tortured and tried for treason.

The execution was brutal and public. Fawkes, already weakened by torture, managed to jump from the scaffold and break his neck, avoiding the gruesome fate of being disembowelled alive. Even so, his body was still mutilated as a warning to others.

Despite his failure, Fawkes has become an enduring symbol of resistance. Every year on November 5th, Britain marks Guy Fawkes Night with fireworks and bonfires, commemorating the plot's failure and celebrating the survival of the monarchy and Parliament.

February 1st

2003 – Space Shuttle Columbia Disintegrates on Reentry, Killing All Seven Crew

On February 1st, 2003, the Space Shuttle Columbia disintegrated as it re-entered Earth's atmosphere, killing all seven astronauts on board. The shuttle had completed a 16-day science mission and was just minutes from landing when disaster struck.

The cause was damage to the thermal protection system, sustained during launch when a piece of foam insulation broke off and struck the shuttle's left wing. The strike went unnoticed during the mission, and when Columbia re-entered the atmosphere, hot gases penetrated the wing, leading to total structural failure.

Debris rained down over Texas and Louisiana. The tragedy shocked the world and led to another suspension of NASA's shuttle program. Investigators later revealed that concerns had been raised during the mission, but the risks were underestimated.

The Columbia disaster, like that of Challenger, forced NASA to once again reevaluate its safety culture and operational procedures. The legacy of the crew lives on through continued space exploration and renewed emphasis on astronaut safety.

February 2nd

1709 – Alexander Selkirk Rescued After Four Years Marooned on a Desert Island

On February 2nd, 1709, Scottish sailor Alexander Selkirk was rescued from Más a Tierra, a remote island in the South Pacific, after surviving alone for over four years. His story of survival later inspired Daniel Defoe's famous novel *Robinson Crusoe*.

Selkirk had been part of a privateering expedition when he argued with his captain about the seaworthiness of their ship. Rather than continue aboard a vessel he feared was doomed, Selkirk asked to be left on the island, believing another ship would come soon. It did not.

Armed with only a musket, a knife, a Bible, and some tools, Selkirk hunted goats, built shelter, and managed to survive. He endured complete isolation, illnesses, and despair. His mental resilience and resourcefulness amazed those who eventually found him.

Selkirk's incredible tale became famous across Europe and served as a testament to the power of human endurance. It also contributed to the romanticised image of the castaway which was a man alone with nature, surviving against the odds.

February 3rd

1959 – "The Day the Music Died": Buddy Holly, Ritchie Valens, and the Big Bopper Die in Plane Crash

On February 3rd, 1959, rock and roll was dealt a devastating blow when a small plane carrying Buddy Holly, Ritchie Valens, and J.P. "The Big Bopper" Richardson crashed in a frozen Iowa cornfield, killing all three musicians and the pilot.

The tour, known as the Winter Dance Party, had been plagued by logistical issues and freezing conditions. Fed up with long, uncomfortable bus rides, Holly chartered a small plane to reach their next venue. Valens and Richardson joined after last-minute seat changes, including a coin toss that Valens won.

Shortly after take-off, the plane encountered poor weather and crashed within minutes. The wreckage was discovered the next morning. The news sent shockwaves across the country. All three were young, talented, and rising stars, especially Holly, who had already left a major mark on the music world.

The event was later immortalised in Don McLean's song "American Pie," which called it "the day the music died." It remains one of the most tragic days in the history of modern music.

February 4th

1945 – Yalta Conference Begins Between Churchill, Roosevelt, and Stalin

On February 4th, 1945, the Yalta Conference began in Crimea, bringing together British Prime Minister Winston Churchill, American President Franklin D. Roosevelt, and Soviet leader Joseph Stalin. This historic summit was a key moment in shaping the post-World War II world.

The war was nearing its end in Europe, and the Allied leaders gathered to discuss how to manage peace, redraw national borders, and address the fate of Nazi Germany. The conference lasted over a week and resulted in several crucial agreements.

Among the decisions made were the division of Germany into occupation zones, the demand for Germany's unconditional surrender, and the agreement to create the United Nations. Stalin also promised free elections in Eastern Europe, though this promise was not kept, leading to future tensions.

Yalta is often viewed as the beginning of the Cold War. Although it marked a moment of cooperation, the seeds of mistrust and geopolitical rivalry between the West and the Soviet Union were clearly present. Its legacy is both significant and deeply controversial.

February 5th

1919 – United Artists Film Studio Founded by Charlie Chaplin and Others

On February 5th, 1919, some of the biggest names in Hollywood made history by taking control of their own creative futures. Charlie Chaplin, Mary Pickford, Douglas Fairbanks, and director D.W. Griffith founded United Artists, a film distribution company that broke with the traditional studio system.

At the time, film studios had total control over actors, directors, and distribution. The founders of United Artists wanted more freedom to make the films they envisioned, without studio interference. Their move was revolutionary, shifting power toward artists rather than corporations.

United Artists helped bring some of the most iconic films of the 20th century to the screen and proved that creative independence could also be commercially successful. It paved the way for future independent filmmaking and empowered generations of directors and performers.

Although the company has gone through numerous changes, buyouts, and rebranding's, the original idea behind it remains a major milestone in film history: that artists should have a say in their own work and profits.

February 6th

1952 – Queen Elizabeth II Becomes Monarch Following the Death of Her Father

On February 6th, 1952, Princess Elizabeth became Queen Elizabeth II after the sudden death of her father, King George VI. She was in Kenya on a royal tour when she learned of his passing, making her the first British monarch in over 200 years to ascend the throne while abroad.

Elizabeth was only 25 years old at the time, and the world was still recovering from World War II. Britain's empire was beginning to shrink, and the modern monarchy faced new challenges. Despite this, her reign would become one of the longest and most stable in British history.

Over the next seventy years, Queen Elizabeth II became a global symbol of continuity, duty, and grace under pressure. She oversaw significant historical events including the end of empire, the Cold War, and dramatic societal changes in the UK.

Her reign left a deep imprint on the monarchy and the world. Her quiet, steadfast leadership helped preserve the relevance of a centuries-old institution in a rapidly changing age.

February 7th

1992 – Signing of the Maastricht Treaty Forms the European Union

On February 7th, 1992, representatives from twelve European countries gathered in the Dutch city of Maastricht to sign one of the most important political agreements in modern history: the Treaty on European Union, commonly known as the Maastricht Treaty.

The treaty laid the foundation for deeper economic and political integration across Europe. It created the European Union as a political entity, established EU citizenship, and outlined plans for a single currency — the euro — which would later be adopted by many member states.

The Maastricht Treaty also defined new areas of cooperation, such as foreign policy, security, and justice. It marked a bold step toward unifying Europe after decades of division, war, and economic rivalry.

However, the treaty was also controversial. Critics argued that it transferred too much power from national governments to Brussels. In the UK, this led to fierce political debates and contributed to the long-term rise of Euroscepticism, culminating in Brexit.

Despite its critics, the Maastricht Treaty remains a landmark in European history.

February 8th

1587 – Mary, Queen of Scots, Executed for Treason

On February 8th, 1587, Mary Stuart, Queen of Scots, was executed at Fotheringhay Castle after being found guilty of plotting to assassinate her cousin, Queen Elizabeth I of England. Her death ended a long and turbulent chapter in British royal history.

Mary had once claimed the English throne herself and was seen as a legitimate Catholic alternative to Protestant Elizabeth. After a series of political missteps, failed marriages, and rebellion, she fled to England seeking protection. Instead, she was imprisoned for 19 years.

Evidence surfaced that Mary had supported the Babington Plot, a plan to kill Elizabeth and place Mary on the throne. The discovery of letters implicating her sealed her fate. Though Elizabeth hesitated to sign the death warrant, political pressure forced her hand.

Mary met her end with dignity, wearing red to symbolise martyrdom. Her execution shocked Europe, especially Catholic powers like Spain. Yet in time, her son James would unite the crowns of Scotland and England, fulfilling the dynastic legacy she never achieved herself.

February 9th

1964 – The Beatles Appear on The Ed Sullivan Show and Spark "Beatlemania" in America

On February 9th, 1964, The Beatles made their American television debut on The Ed Sullivan Show, performing live to an estimated 73 million viewers. That single appearance changed the landscape of popular music forever.

John Lennon, Paul McCartney, George Harrison, and Ringo Starr had already taken Britain by storm. Now, they were ready to conquer America. Their charm, energy, and catchy songs captivated the audience, especially teenagers. The studio was filled with screaming fans, and the Beatles' performance became a cultural moment.

The band performed five songs, including "All My Loving" and "I Want to Hold Your Hand." Overnight, they became household names in the United States. Their success launched the British Invasion, opening the doors for other UK acts to dominate American charts.

The Beatles didn't just change music — they transformed fashion, youth culture, and even global politics in subtle ways. Their Ed Sullivan debut remains one of the most iconic moments in entertainment history.

February 10th

1763 – Treaty of Paris Signed, Ending the Seven Years' War

On February 10th, 1763, the Treaty of Paris was signed by Britain, France, and Spain, officially ending the Seven Years' War. This global conflict, which had raged since 1756, involved almost every major European power and reshaped the balance of power across continents.

The treaty was a decisive victory for Britain. France ceded most of its North American territories, including Canada and lands east of the Mississippi River, to Britain. Spain gave up Florida in exchange for French lands west of the Mississippi. France retained some Caribbean islands and fishing rights near Newfoundland, but its presence in North America was effectively ended.

The treaty redrew maps and laid the groundwork for future colonial and national tensions. In North America, British dominance grew, but so did unrest among the colonists who would later rebel in the American Revolution.

Though often overshadowed by later wars, the Seven Years' War was truly global and its conclusion in 1763 marked the beginning of a new imperial age.

February 11th

1990 – Nelson Mandela Is Freed After 27 Years in Prison

On February 11th, 1990, Nelson Mandela walked out of Victor Verster Prison in South Africa, a free man after 27 years behind bars. His release was broadcast live around the world and symbolised the beginning of the end for the apartheid regime.

Mandela had been imprisoned in 1962 for his role in fighting the apartheid government, which enforced a brutal system of racial segregation. He spent 18 years on Robben Island before being moved to other prisons, becoming a global symbol of resistance.

His release came after years of internal protests, international pressure, and secret negotiations. South African President F.W. de Klerk had recently unbanned the African National Congress and promised reforms. Mandela emerged calm and determined, calling for peace and reconciliation rather than revenge.

Four years later, Mandela would become South Africa's first Black president in a democratic election. His release is widely seen as a turning point in one of the most remarkable political transitions of the 20th century.

February 12th

1809 – Charles Darwin Is Born in England

On February 12th, 1809, Charles Robert Darwin was born in Shrewsbury, England. He would go on to become one of the most influential scientists in history, fundamentally changing how humanity understands life on Earth.

Darwin's most famous work, *On the Origin of Species*, published in 1859, introduced the theory of evolution by natural selection. He proposed that species evolve over time through a process of survival and reproduction of the fittest traits. This idea challenged traditional beliefs and sparked fierce debate in both scientific and religious circles.

His groundbreaking research was based on observations made during a five-year voyage aboard HMS Beagle, especially in the Galápagos Islands. There, he noticed subtle differences among species that hinted at adaptation and change over generations.

Today, Darwin's theory remains a cornerstone of modern biology. His legacy lives on not only in science but also in education, philosophy, and our understanding of the natural world.

February 13th

1945 – Allied Bombing of Dresden Begins During World War II

On February 13th, 1945, Allied forces launched a massive bombing campaign on the German city of Dresden, unleashing one of the most controversial air raids of World War II. Over the next three days, the city was devastated and tens of thousands of civilians were killed.

Dresden had been largely untouched by previous bombings and was known for its historic architecture and cultural significance. The British Royal Air Force and the United States Army Air Forces dropped more than 3,900 tons of explosives and incendiary devices on the city, creating a firestorm that destroyed large parts of the urban centre.

The attack was intended to demoralise the German population and disrupt transportation and military communication. However, critics have long argued that Dresden had little military value and that the bombing was disproportionate to any strategic gain.

The death toll is estimated between 25,000 and 35,000. The bombing of Dresden remains a subject of debate, raising difficult questions about wartime ethics and the cost of total war.

February 14th

1929 – The Saint Valentine's Day Massacre Shocks Chicago

On February 14th, 1929, one of the most infamous gangland killings in American history occurred in Chicago. Known as the Saint Valentine's Day Massacre, it was the peak of a bloody turf war between rival bootlegging gangs during Prohibition.

Seven members and associates of George "Bugs" Moran's gang were lined up against a wall in a North Side garage and gunned down by men posing as police officers. The attackers were believed to be linked to Al Capone's South Side gang, though Capone himself was in Florida at the time and never formally charged.

The massacre shocked the nation and highlighted the extreme violence that accompanied the illegal alcohol trade. It also drew greater attention to organised crime and corruption in American cities.

The brutality of the killings — all victims shot at close range with tommy guns — made headlines across the country. The event helped tarnish Capone's image and increased public pressure to crack down on mob violence and Prohibition.

February 15th

1564 – Galileo Galilei Is Born in Pisa, Italy

On February 15th, 1564, Galileo Galilei was born in Pisa, Italy. He would grow to become one of the most important figures in the history of science, helping to lay the foundation for modern physics and astronomy.

Galileo championed the use of observation and experimentation at a time when scientific inquiry was heavily influenced by tradition and authority. He improved the telescope and used it to make astonishing discoveries, including the moons of Jupiter, the phases of Venus, and the rough surface of the Moon.

His support for the Copernican model, which placed the Sun at the centre of the solar system, brought him into direct conflict with the Catholic Church. In 1633, he was tried for heresy and forced to recant, spending the rest of his life under house arrest.

Despite this, his work continued to influence generations of scientists. Galileo is often called the "father of modern science" and is remembered for his courage, curiosity, and commitment to truth.

February 16th

1923 – Howard Carter Opens the Burial Chamber of King Tutankhamun

On February 16th, 1923, British archaeologist Howard Carter officially opened the sealed burial chamber of Pharaoh Tutankhamun in Egypt's Valley of the Kings. It was one of the most extraordinary archaeological discoveries of the 20th century.

Carter had first discovered the tomb in November 1922, but it took months to carefully excavate and document the incredible finds. When the burial chamber was opened, it revealed treasures unlike anything seen before: golden shrines, statues, jewellery, and most famously, the pharaoh's golden sarcophagus and death mask.

Tutankhamun had died young and ruled during a relatively unremarkable period, but the untouched nature of his tomb provided an unprecedented glimpse into ancient Egyptian burial practices.

The discovery sparked worldwide fascination and a revival of interest in ancient Egypt. It also fed popular legends, including the so-called "curse of the pharaohs," after several people involved in the dig died under mysterious circumstances. Regardless of the myths, the tomb's impact on archaeology and history is undeniable.

February 17th

1600 – Philosopher Giordano Bruno Is Executed for Heresy in Rome

On February 17th, 1600, Italian philosopher and former Dominican friar Giordano Bruno was burned at the stake in Rome after being convicted of heresy by the Roman Catholic Inquisition. His execution remains one of the most dramatic clashes between free thought and religious orthodoxy in history.

Bruno held radical views for his time. He believed the universe was infinite and that stars were distant suns with their own planets. He rejected the idea of a single, central Earth and supported a form of cosmic pluralism. These ideas challenged both scientific and theological doctrines.

Bruno's defiance went beyond astronomy. He also questioned the divinity of Christ and the authority of the Church. After eight years of imprisonment and interrogation, he was found guilty and executed in the Campo de' Fiori.

Centuries later, Bruno became a symbol of intellectual freedom and the high cost of pursuing truth against dominant ideologies. A statue in the square where he died now honours his legacy.

February 18th

1930 – Pluto Is Discovered by Clyde Tombaugh

On February 18th, 1930, 24-year-old astronomer Clyde Tombaugh discovered Pluto at the Lowell Observatory in Flagstaff, Arizona. It was the first object to be identified in what would later be called the Kuiper Belt.

Tombaugh was systematically examining the night sky using photographic plates when he noticed a faint, slow-moving dot. Further analysis confirmed it was a new celestial body, and it was soon named Pluto, after the Roman god of the underworld. The name was suggested by an 11-year-old English girl, Venetia Burney.

At the time, Pluto was hailed as the ninth planet in the Solar System, though its small size and unusual orbit puzzled astronomers. In 2006, it was reclassified as a "dwarf planet," a move that sparked public debate and nostalgia.

Despite the reclassification, Pluto remains one of the most fascinating objects in space. NASA's New Horizons mission, which flew past it in 2015, revealed a world of icy mountains, vast plains, and mysterious geological activity.

February 19th

1942 – Japanese-American Internment Ordered in the United States

On February 19th, 1942, U.S. President Franklin D. Roosevelt signed Executive Order 9066, authorising the forced relocation and internment of over 120,000 Japanese-Americans. The order was issued just months after the attack on Pearl Harbor and remains one of the most controversial decisions in American wartime history.

Those affected were mostly American citizens living on the West Coast. They were given days to pack and were sent to remote internment camps under armed guard. Families lost homes, businesses, and possessions with little or no compensation.

The government claimed the action was a military necessity, but no cases of espionage or sabotage by Japanese-Americans were ever proven. The policy was widely criticised at the time and even more so in the decades that followed.

In 1988, the U.S. government formally apologised and paid reparations to surviving internees. The episode is now viewed as a grave violation of civil liberties rooted in fear and racial prejudice.

February 20th

1962 – John Glenn Becomes First American to Orbit the Earth

On February 20th, 1962, astronaut John Glenn made history when he became the first American to orbit the Earth. Aboard the spacecraft *Friendship 7*, he completed three orbits in just under five hours.

The mission was a critical milestone in the Cold War space race. The Soviet Union had already sent Yuri Gagarin into orbit in 1961, and Glenn's successful flight helped restore American confidence and momentum.

Glenn faced challenges during the flight, including a potential issue with the heat shield that led to intense concern during re-entry. Despite the risks, he splashed down safely in the Atlantic Ocean and was celebrated as a national hero.

His achievement paved the way for future NASA missions and eventual moon landings. Decades later, Glenn returned to space in 1998 at the age of 77, becoming the oldest person to fly in space at the time. His life embodied courage, service, and exploration.

February 21st

1848 – The Communist Manifesto Is Published by Marx and Engels

On February 21st, 1848, Karl Marx and Friedrich Engels published *The Communist Manifesto*, a short but powerful political pamphlet that would become one of the most influential texts in modern history.

The manifesto argued that all of history was shaped by class struggle and that the working class, or proletariat, should rise up against the ruling bourgeoisie. It called for the abolition of private property, the end of capitalism, and the creation of a classless society.

Written on the eve of widespread European revolutions, the manifesto captured the growing unrest among workers. Though largely ignored at first, it gained traction over the following decades and inspired socialist and communist movements around the world.

Its famous opening line, "A spectre is haunting Europe," and closing call, "Workers of the world, unite!" became rallying cries. Whether praised or criticised, the influence of the manifesto cannot be overstated. It helped shape revolutions, governments, and ideological conflicts for over a century.

February 22nd

1943 – White Rose Resistance Members Executed in Nazi Germany

On February 22nd, 1943, Hans and Sophie Scholl, along with their friend Christoph Probst, were executed in Munich for their role in the White Rose resistance group. They were among the few Germans who publicly opposed Hitler during the height of World War II.

The White Rose was a small student-led movement based at the University of Munich. Its members secretly distributed leaflets denouncing the Nazi regime, calling for nonviolent resistance and an end to the war. The group's courage was exceptional in a country ruled by fear and propaganda.

The Scholls were arrested after being caught distributing leaflets on campus. In a swift show trial, they were sentenced to death for treason and beheaded hours later. Their bravery and moral clarity stood in stark contrast to the brutality of the regime.

Today, the White Rose is remembered as a symbol of conscience and courage. Their final words were a message of hope: "Long live freedom!"

February 23rd

1945 – U.S. Marines Raise the Flag on Iwo Jima

On February 23rd, 1945, during one of the fiercest battles of World War II, five U.S. Marines and a Navy corpsman raised the American flag atop Mount Suribachi on the Japanese island of Iwo Jima. The moment was captured in a photograph by Joe Rosenthal that became one of the most iconic images of the war.

The Battle of Iwo Jima had begun just five days earlier, with the objective of capturing the island's airfields and gaining a strategic base near Japan. The fighting was brutal, with heavily fortified Japanese defences and underground tunnels turning the island into a deadly maze.

The flag-raising came after the capture of the mountain's summit, providing a much-needed morale boost for American forces. Though the photo is often seen as the end of the battle, intense fighting continued for nearly a month more.

Of the six men in the photograph, three were killed before the battle ended. The image became a symbol of sacrifice, resilience, and victory, later memorialised in statues and stamps across the United States.

February 24th

1582 – Pope Gregory XIII Introduces the Gregorian Calendar

On February 24th, 1582, Pope Gregory XIII issued the papal bull *Inter gravissimas*, reforming the Julian calendar and introducing what is now known as the Gregorian calendar. This change corrected significant inaccuracies in how time had been measured for over a millennium.

The Julian calendar, introduced by Julius Caesar in 46 BC, miscalculated the length of a solar year by about 11 minutes. Over centuries, this small error accumulated, throwing the date of Easter and other important Christian holidays out of alignment with the seasons.

To fix the issue, ten days were dropped from the calendar in October 1582, and a new system was established where leap years occurred more precisely. The reform kept the calendar better aligned with the Earth's revolutions around the sun.

Catholic countries adopted the new calendar almost immediately, while Protestant and Orthodox nations resisted the change for years or even centuries. Today, the Gregorian calendar is the most widely used civil calendar in the world.

February 25th

1836 – Samuel Colt Receives Patent for His Revolver

On February 25th, 1836, Samuel Colt was granted a U.S. patent for his revolutionary invention: the Colt revolver. This firearm, capable of firing multiple rounds without reloading, would go on to change the face of warfare, law enforcement, and the American frontier.

Colt's design used a rotating cylinder with multiple chambers, allowing users to fire several shots in quick succession. At a time when most guns had to be manually reloaded after each shot, the Colt revolver offered a powerful advantage in speed and efficiency.

Although his early attempts to sell the weapon met with limited success, the outbreak of the Mexican-American War and later the American Civil War brought massive demand. Colt's factory in Hartford, Connecticut, became one of the first to use mass production techniques effectively.

The Colt revolver became a symbol of the American West, carried by cowboys, outlaws, and lawmen alike. Samuel Colt's invention not only changed firearms but also helped shape American industry and legend.

February 26th

1993 – World Trade Centre Bombed in New York City

On February 26th, 1993, a powerful truck bomb exploded beneath the North Tower of the World Trade Centre in New York City. The attack killed six people, injured over a thousand, and marked one of the first major acts of terrorism on American soil.

The bomb, made from over a thousand pounds of urea nitrate and hydrogen gas, was placed in a rental van and detonated in the underground parking garage. The explosion created a crater several stories deep and knocked out power and communications for the complex.

The attack was orchestrated by a group of Islamic extremists, including Ramzi Yousef, who planned to bring down both towers by collapsing one into the other. Though the plan failed, the incident shocked the nation and revealed the growing threat of international terrorism.

Security measures were tightened in the aftermath, but the full implications would not be understood until the attacks of September 11th, 2001. The 1993 bombing is now seen as a chilling precursor to that later tragedy.

February 27th

1933 – Reichstag Fire Used to Consolidate Nazi Power in Germany

On February 27th, 1933, the Reichstag building, home of the German parliament in Berlin, was set ablaze. The fire was quickly blamed on communists and was used by Adolf Hitler's government as a pretext to suspend civil liberties and eliminate political opposition.

A Dutch communist named Marinus van der Lubbe was arrested at the scene and later executed, though many historians believe the Nazis may have orchestrated or exploited the fire themselves. The next day, President Paul von Hindenburg signed the Reichstag Fire Decree at Hitler's urging.

This decree suspended key civil rights such as freedom of speech, assembly, and the press. It also allowed for indefinite detention without trial. Thousands of communists, socialists, and other opponents of the regime were arrested in the days that followed.

The fire marked a turning point in Germany's descent into dictatorship. Just a month later, Hitler passed the Enabling Act, giving him absolute power. The Reichstag fire remains one of the most pivotal and controversial events in 20th-century political history.

February 28th

1953 – Structure of DNA Discovered by Watson and Crick

On February 28th, 1953, James Watson and Francis Crick made a breakthrough that would revolutionise biology. At the Cavendish Laboratory in Cambridge, they discovered the double helix structure of DNA, the molecule that carries genetic information in living organisms.

The discovery was based on years of research by many scientists, including Rosalind Franklin and Maurice Wilkins, whose X-ray diffraction images of DNA provided crucial evidence. Using a combination of model-building and existing data, Watson and Crick determined that DNA consists of two intertwined strands held together by base pairs.

Their findings were published in *Nature* in April 1953 and earned them a Nobel Prize in 1962. The double helix model explained how genetic information is copied and passed down, laying the groundwork for modern genetics, biotechnology, and medicine.

The discovery of DNA's structure remains one of the greatest scientific achievements of the 20th century, unlocking the secrets of heredity and transforming our understanding of life itself.

February 29th (had to include it didn't I)

1940 – Hattie McDaniel Becomes First African American to Win an Oscar

On February 29th, 1940, actress Hattie McDaniel made history at the 12th Academy Awards by becoming the first African American to win an Oscar. She received the Best Supporting Actress award for her role as Mammy in *Gone with the Wind*.

Her win was a major milestone, but it came with contradictions. McDaniel was not allowed to sit with the main cast at the segregated ceremony held at the Ambassador Hotel in Los Angeles. Despite her success, she continued to face discrimination in Hollywood and was often limited to servant roles.

Nonetheless, McDaniel used her platform to push for greater representation and opportunities for Black performers. She remained proud of her work and famously said, "I'd rather play a maid than be one."

Her award paved the way for future generations of Black actors and remains a symbol of both progress and the enduring struggles for racial equality in the entertainment industry.

March 1st

1872 – Yellowstone Becomes the First National Park

On March 1st, 1872, U.S. President Ulysses S. Grant signed a law establishing Yellowstone National Park, making it the first national park in the world. Located primarily in Wyoming, Yellowstone was set aside to preserve its unique geothermal features, wildlife, and natural beauty for public enjoyment.

The park covers over 2 million acres and includes geysers, hot springs, canyons, rivers, and forests. It is home to grizzly bears, wolves, bison, and elk, among many other species. Its most famous feature, Old Faithful, is a geyser that regularly erupts with steaming jets of water.

The creation of Yellowstone set a precedent for conservation around the globe. The idea that natural wonders should be protected by government for future generations was groundbreaking at the time.

Today, the U.S. National Park Service oversees more than 400 sites across the country. Yellowstone remains a crown jewel and a testament to early efforts in environmental stewardship.

March 2nd

1836 – Texas Declares Independence from Mexico

On March 2nd, 1836, delegates at the Convention of 1836 adopted the Texas Declaration of Independence, officially severing ties with Mexico and forming the Republic of Texas. The declaration was signed at Washington-on-the-Brazos, as Mexican forces laid siege to the Alamo.

Tensions between Anglo-American settlers and the Mexican government had been growing for years, especially over issues like immigration, religion, and slavery. Under the leadership of figures such as Sam Houston and Stephen F. Austin, Texans sought autonomy and eventually full independence.

The fight for independence was hard-fought and bloody. The fall of the Alamo and the massacre at Goliad fueled determination among Texans, leading to a decisive victory at the Battle of San Jacinto in April.

Texas remained an independent republic until 1845, when it was annexed by the United States. Its brief independence left a lasting legacy, and the date is still celebrated annually as Texas Independence Day.

March 3rd

1931 – "The Star-Spangled Banner" Becomes the U.S. National Anthem

On March 3rd, 1931, President Herbert Hoover signed a congressional resolution officially designating "The Star-Spangled Banner" as the national anthem of the United States. The lyrics were written by Francis Scott Key during the War of 1812.

Key penned the poem in 1814 after witnessing the British bombardment of Fort McHenry in Baltimore. Inspired by the sight of the American flag still flying at dawn, he wrote verses that were later set to the tune of a popular British song.

Although it had been widely used for decades, the song had never been formally adopted. Efforts to recognise it as the anthem gained momentum in the 1920s, particularly from veterans' groups.

The anthem has since become a defining symbol of American identity, performed at public events, sports games, and national ceremonies. Its lyrics, filled with hope and resilience, continue to resonate nearly two centuries after they were written.

March 4th

1933 – Franklin D. Roosevelt Inaugurated Amid the Great Depression

On March 4th, 1933, Franklin D. Roosevelt was inaugurated as the 32nd President of the United States during the depths of the Great Depression. His inauguration speech famously declared, "The only thing we have to fear is fear itself."

America was facing unprecedented economic hardship. Banks were collapsing, unemployment was sky-high, and public confidence was at an all-time low. Roosevelt's speech inspired hope and signalled a bold new approach.

He quickly launched the New Deal, a sweeping series of programs aimed at relief, recovery, and reform. These included Social Security, public works projects, financial regulations, and efforts to stabilise the banking system.

FDR's presidency redefined the role of the federal government and transformed American politics. He would go on to be elected four times, guiding the nation through both economic depression and global war.

March 5th

1953 – Joseph Stalin Dies, Ending a Brutal Soviet Era

On March 5th, 1953, Soviet leader Joseph Stalin died after suffering a stroke, marking the end of a reign defined by terror, repression, and immense power. His death sparked mourning, confusion, and a significant power struggle within the USSR.

Stalin had ruled with an iron fist since the 1920s, consolidating power after Lenin's death. He launched industrialisation campaigns, purged political rivals, and oversaw the deaths of millions through forced famines, gulags, and state terror.

Though he played a major role in defeating Nazi Germany during World War II, his legacy was deeply controversial. Fear permeated Soviet life, and dissent was crushed brutally.

After his death, the Soviet Union gradually moved into a period of de-Stalinisation under Nikita Khrushchev, who denounced Stalin's cult of personality. The transition helped thaw some of the Cold War tensions but left a lasting scar on Russian history.

March 6th

1899 – Aspirin Is Patented by Bayer

On March 6th, 1899, the German pharmaceutical company Bayer received a patent for acetylsalicylic acid, a compound it marketed as "Aspirin." It would go on to become one of the most widely used medications in the world.

Derived from compounds found in willow bark, aspirin was developed in a more stable form by Bayer chemist Felix Hoffmann. It was originally intended as a treatment for pain and inflammation, and quickly became popular across Europe and America.

Aspirin's usefulness expanded over time. Doctors discovered its ability to reduce fever, thin the blood, and lower the risk of heart attacks and strokes. Its influence on medicine has been profound.

Though Bayer lost the trademark after World War I, the drug itself became a household name. Aspirin's long history as a cheap, effective, and versatile medication has earned it a permanent place in medical history.

March 7th

1876 – Alexander Graham Bell Receives Patent for the Telephone

On March 7th, 1876, Alexander Graham Bell received U.S. Patent No. 174,465 for an invention that would change the world: the telephone. His device transmitted speech electronically, allowing real-time communication over distances.

Bell had been experimenting with ways to improve the telegraph when he and his assistant, Thomas Watson, stumbled on a method to convert sound waves into electrical signals. Just days after receiving the patent, Bell made the first successful telephone call with the words, "Mr. Watson, come here. I want to see you."

The invention was met with scepticism at first, but its revolutionary potential quickly became clear. Bell went on to form the Bell Telephone Company, which eventually evolved into AT&T.

The telephone transformed global communication, making instant connection possible across towns, countries, and eventually continents. Bell's invention paved the way for the digital age we live in today.

March 8th

1917 – Russian Revolution Begins with Women's Protest in Petrograd

On March 8th, 1917, a massive protest led by women in Petrograd (now Saint Petersburg) marked the beginning of the Russian Revolution. Striking over food shortages, working conditions, and political repression, the protest rapidly grew into a nationwide uprising.

The demonstration coincided with International Women's Day and quickly attracted thousands of workers and soldiers. What began as a peaceful protest became a full-scale rebellion against Tsar Nicholas II, whose government was already weakened by years of war and economic crisis.

Within a week, the tsar abdicated, ending centuries of Romanov rule. A provisional government took power, but it too would be overthrown later that year in the Bolshevik Revolution led by Lenin.

The events of March 1917 changed the course of Russian and world history, setting the stage for the rise of communism and the Soviet Union.

March 9th

1959 – Barbie Doll Debuts at the American International Toy Fair

On March 9th, 1959, the first Barbie doll was unveiled by the Mattel toy company at the American International Toy Fair in New York City. Created by Ruth Handler, Barbie was designed to be a teenage fashion model, breaking away from the traditional baby dolls that dominated the market at the time.

Ruth Handler got the idea after observing her daughter, Barbara, playing with paper dolls and imagining adult lives for them. She believed girls wanted a doll that allowed them to dream about the future. Named after her daughter, Barbie came dressed in a black-and-white striped swimsuit, with blonde ponytail and high heels.

The initial reaction to Barbie was mixed, with some parents concerned about her figure. But the doll quickly became a bestseller and evolved into a global icon. Over the decades, Barbie has had over 200 careers and reflected cultural changes, from astronaut to presidential candidate.

Barbie has also faced criticism over body image and gender roles but has continually adapted to include diverse body types, ethnicities, and backgrounds. Today, Barbie remains a powerful cultural symbol and one of the most successful toys ever made.

March 10th

1876 – First Successful Telephone Call Made by Alexander Graham Bell

On March 10th, 1876, Alexander Graham Bell made the world's first successful telephone call. Speaking to his assistant Thomas Watson in another room, he famously said, "Mr. Watson, come here. I want to see you." The words marked a turning point in human communication.

Bell and Watson had been working on devices that could transmit vocal sounds electronically. Just three days earlier, Bell had secured a patent for his invention. The March 10th breakthrough proved that intelligible speech could travel via electrical wires.

Though rudimentary, the invention would soon evolve and become commercially viable. Bell demonstrated the phone at expositions and quickly gained support. The Bell Telephone Company was founded in 1877 and laid the groundwork for the modern telecommunications industry.

The success of this first call revolutionised the way people connected over distance. It changed business, personal communication, and global society. What started as a wire and diaphragm now connects billions of people in real time across the world.

March 11th

2011 – Japan Hit by Devastating Earthquake and Tsunami

On March 11th, 2011, a powerful 9.0-magnitude undersea earthquake struck off the northeast coast of Honshu, Japan, triggering a massive tsunami that devastated coastal areas and caused the worst nuclear disaster since Chernobyl.

The quake was one of the strongest ever recorded, and the resulting tsunami reached heights of up to 40 meters in some areas. Entire towns were swept away, and over 15,000 people were confirmed dead, with thousands more missing or injured.

In addition to the human tragedy, the tsunami disabled power and cooling systems at the Fukushima Daiichi Nuclear Power Plant, leading to three reactor meltdowns. Radioactive material was released into the air and ocean, forcing the evacuation of hundreds of thousands of residents.

The disaster prompted widespread reassessment of nuclear safety worldwide and caused Japan to shut down many of its reactors. Recovery and cleanup efforts continue more than a decade later.

The 2011 Tōhoku disaster remains a stark reminder of nature's power and the importance of disaster preparedness in a highly populated, technologically advanced world.

March 12th

1930 – Gandhi Begins the Salt March in India

On March 12th, 1930, Mahatma Gandhi began the Salt March, a pivotal act of nonviolent protest against British colonial rule in India. The 240-mile journey from Sabarmati Ashram to the coastal village of Dandi challenged the British monopoly on salt production and taxation.

At the time, it was illegal for Indians to produce or collect their own salt, forcing them to buy heavily taxed British salt. Gandhi saw this as a symbol of broader oppression. He set off with 78 followers, but thousands joined along the way.

After 24 days, Gandhi reached the sea and symbolically gathered salt from the shore, breaking the law. The act ignited a nationwide civil disobedience movement. Over 60,000 people were arrested, including Gandhi himself.

The Salt March captured international attention and marked a turning point in the Indian independence movement. It demonstrated the power of nonviolent resistance and inspired future civil rights leaders around the world.

March 13th

1881 – Tsar Alexander II of Russia Assassinated in St. Petersburg

On March 13th, 1881, Russian Tsar Alexander II was assassinated by members of the radical group People's Will in St. Petersburg. He was killed by a bomb thrown as his carriage passed near the Winter Palace, just hours after he had signed plans for a national assembly.

Alexander II is remembered for emancipating the serfs in 1861, a landmark reform that aimed to modernise Russia. He also implemented judicial and military changes and expanded educational opportunities. Yet his reign faced increasing opposition from revolutionaries who saw him as too slow or insincere in reform.

On the day of his assassination, the first bomb damaged his carriage but left him unharmed. When he got out to check on the wounded, a second bomber threw another explosive, killing the tsar instantly.

His death plunged Russia into political reaction and repression. His successor, Alexander III, rolled back many reforms. The event marked a key moment in Russian revolutionary history and foreshadowed the eventual collapse of the Romanov dynasty.

March 14th

1879 – Birth of Albert Einstein, Revolutionary Theoretical Physicist

On March 14th, 1879, Albert Einstein was born in Ulm, in the Kingdom of Württemberg, Germany. He would grow up to become one of the most influential scientists in history, transforming our understanding of time, space, and energy.

Einstein showed early signs of brilliance, but his academic journey was not always smooth. He eventually studied physics in Switzerland and developed groundbreaking ideas while working as a patent clerk. In 1905, he published his theory of special relativity, introducing the famous equation $E = mc^2$.

Later, in 1915, Einstein unveiled his general theory of relativity, revolutionising the way scientists viewed gravity. His predictions were confirmed by astronomical observations, and he quickly became a global icon.

Einstein was also a committed pacifist, a refugee from Nazi Germany, and a public intellectual who warned of the dangers of nuclear weapons. He spent his later years in the United States at Princeton University.

Albert Einstein's legacy continues to shape physics, philosophy, and the popular imagination.

March 15th

44 BC – Julius Caesar Assassinated on the Ides of March

On March 15th, 44 BC, Roman dictator Julius Caesar was assassinated by a group of senators in the Theatre of Pompey in Rome. The day, known as the Ides of March, became one of the most famous dates in history.

Caesar had recently declared himself dictator for life, alarming many senators who feared he was dismantling the republic to become a monarch. Led by Brutus, Cassius, and other conspirators, the senators stabbed Caesar 23 times during a meeting, believing they were saving the republic.

However, the murder plunged Rome into a new series of civil wars. Rather than restoring the republic, the assassination cleared the way for Caesar's heir, Octavian (later Augustus), to become the first Roman emperor.

The phrase "Beware the Ides of March," from Shakespeare's play *Julius Caesar*, has become a cultural warning about betrayal and political intrigue. Caesar's death marked the end of the Roman Republic and the birth of the Roman Empire.

March 16th

1968 – My Lai Massacre Occurs During the Vietnam War

On March 16th, 1968, American soldiers from Charlie Company, 11th Infantry Brigade, massacred over 500 unarmed Vietnamese civilians in the hamlet of My Lai. Most of the victims were women, children, and elderly men.

The troops had been ordered to engage suspected Viet Cong fighters in the area, but they found no armed resistance. Instead, under the command of Lieutenant William Calley, they carried out brutal killings, rapes, and the destruction of the village.

The massacre was initially covered up by the military but was later exposed by whistleblowers, journalists, and an internal investigation. The revelation sparked outrage and further eroded public support for the war.

Calley was the only soldier convicted, receiving a life sentence that was later reduced to house arrest. The My Lai Massacre remains a dark chapter in U.S. military history and a symbol of the horrors of war and moral failure.

March 17th

461 – Death of Saint Patrick, Patron Saint of Ireland

On March 17th, 461, Saint Patrick, the most famous patron saint of Ireland, is believed to have died. The date later became known as St. Patrick's Day, a national holiday in Ireland and a global celebration of Irish heritage.

Born in Roman Britain in the late 4th century, Patrick was kidnapped by Irish raiders and enslaved as a shepherd in Ireland. After six years, he escaped and returned home, only to later come back to Ireland as a Christian missionary.

Patrick is credited with converting much of Ireland to Christianity, using symbols like the shamrock to explain the Holy Trinity. Although some stories, like his driving out of snakes, are mythological, his influence on Irish culture and identity is profound.

Today, St. Patrick's Day is celebrated with parades, music, and festivals across the world, especially in countries with large Irish diasporas. It honours a man whose real and legendary deeds left a lasting spiritual legacy.

March 18th

1965 – First Spacewalk Performed by Alexei Leonov

On March 18th, 1965, Soviet cosmonaut Alexei Leonov became the first person to walk in space. During the Voskhod 2 mission, he exited the spacecraft and floated in space for 12 minutes, connected only by a tether.

The event was a major milestone in the space race between the United States and the Soviet Union. Leonov's spacewalk demonstrated human ability to survive and work outside a spacecraft, an essential step for future moon missions and space stations.

The mission was not without danger. Leonov's spacesuit expanded in the vacuum of space, making it difficult to re-enter the airlock. He had to bleed off pressure manually, risking his life in the process.

Despite the peril, Leonov's spacewalk was a triumph for Soviet space exploration and a testament to human courage. It paved the way for all future extravehicular activities and remains a historic moment in the conquest of space.

March 19th

2003 – U.S. Begins Invasion of Iraq

On March 19th, 2003, the United States and coalition forces launched a military invasion of Iraq, beginning with an airstrike on Baghdad and followed by a ground assault. The goal, according to U.S. President George W. Bush, was to disarm Iraq of weapons of mass destruction and remove Saddam Hussein from power.

The operation, dubbed "shock and awe," involved massive bombing campaigns. Within weeks, Baghdad fell, and Saddam's regime collapsed. However, no weapons of mass destruction were found, leading to widespread controversy.

The war triggered a prolonged and bloody insurgency, sectarian violence, and a humanitarian crisis. It also strained U.S. alliances and reshaped Middle Eastern politics. Saddam Hussein was eventually captured, tried, and executed in 2006.

The Iraq War remains one of the most debated conflicts of the 21st century, with questions over intelligence failures, political motives, and the long-term consequences of intervention.

March 20th

1852 – Harriet Beecher Stowe Publishes *Uncle Tom's Cabin*

On March 20th, 1852, American author Harriet Beecher Stowe published *Uncle Tom's Cabin*, a powerful anti-slavery novel that electrified public opinion and helped fuel the abolitionist movement in the United States.

The book tells the story of Uncle Tom, a long-suffering Black slave, and the brutality he and other characters endure under slavery. Drawing on firsthand accounts and religious convictions, Stowe portrayed the institution as morally evil and dehumanising.

The novel sold over 300,000 copies in its first year and became one of the most influential books in American history. It deeply affected readers in the North and provoked outrage in the South, where it was banned in some areas.

When Abraham Lincoln met Stowe during the Civil War, he is said to have remarked, "So you're the little woman who wrote the book that started this great war." Whether apocryphal or not, the story highlights the novel's impact on a divided nation.

March 21st

1960 – Sharpeville Massacre in South Africa

On March 21st, 1960, South African police opened fire on a crowd of peaceful Black protesters in the township of Sharpeville, killing 69 people and wounding over 180. The demonstrators were protesting apartheid pass laws, which restricted movement and required Black South Africans to carry identification at all times.

Organised by the Pan Africanist Congress, the protest called on people to surrender their pass books and submit to arrest in defiance of the law. When a crowd of thousands gathered outside the police station, officers panicked and began shooting into the unarmed group.

The massacre shocked the world and intensified international condemnation of apartheid. In response, the South African government banned anti-apartheid organisations and cracked down on dissent. Nelson Mandela and other leaders would later cite Sharpeville as a turning point in the struggle.

Today, March 21st is commemorated as Human Rights Day in South Africa, in honour of those who lost their lives in the fight for freedom.

March 22nd

1765 – British Parliament Passes the Stamp Act

On March 22nd, 1765, the British Parliament passed the Stamp Act, a tax measure that would inflame colonial anger and help spark the American Revolution. The law required that printed materials in the American colonies, such as newspapers, legal documents, and playing cards, carry a special tax stamp.

The tax was designed to help pay for British troops stationed in North America following the Seven Years' War. But many colonists viewed it as a violation of their rights, arguing they should not be taxed without representation in Parliament.

Protests erupted across the colonies. Merchants organised boycotts, and groups like the Sons of Liberty formed to resist enforcement. The backlash was so strong that the Act was repealed a year later.

Though short-lived, the Stamp Act set a precedent for colonial unity and resistance. It was a key step on the road to independence and helped shape the revolutionary spirit that would culminate a decade later in the Declaration of Independence.

March 23rd

1775 – Patrick Henry Delivers His "Give Me Liberty or Give Me Death" Speech

On March 23rd, 1775, American statesman Patrick Henry delivered one of the most famous speeches in U.S. history at the Virginia Convention in Richmond. In a fiery call to arms against British rule, Henry closed with the immortal words, "Give me liberty, or give me death!"

Tensions between the American colonies and the British government were escalating rapidly. While some delegates still hoped for peaceful resolution, Henry argued that war was inevitable and urged immediate preparation for conflict.

The speech was not officially recorded at the time, but it was remembered and reconstructed later by Henry's biographer. Its power lay in its emotional appeal, passion, and patriotic fervour. Henry's words helped to galvanise support for the revolutionary cause in Virginia and beyond.

The following month, fighting broke out at Lexington and Concord, marking the beginning of the American Revolutionary War. Patrick Henry's defiant message remains a powerful symbol of the desire for freedom in the face of tyranny.

March 24th

1603 – Queen Elizabeth I of England Dies, Ending the Tudor Dynasty

On March 24th, 1603, Queen Elizabeth I of England died at Richmond Palace at the age of 69, ending the Tudor dynasty and bringing in the Stuart era under King James VI of Scotland. Her death marked the close of one of the most celebrated reigns in English history.

Elizabeth had ruled for 44 years during a period known as the Elizabethan Age, a time of cultural flourishing, maritime exploration, and relative internal peace. She navigated religious conflict, defeated the Spanish Armada in 1588, and presided over a court that nurtured William Shakespeare and other great artists.

Despite numerous suitors, Elizabeth never married and was known as the "Virgin Queen." Her refusal to name a clear successor caused anxiety toward the end of her reign, but her cousin James VI of Scotland ascended the throne smoothly, becoming James I of England.

Elizabeth's legacy lives on in her image as a wise and powerful monarch who stabilised England and helped shape its national identity.

March 25th

1911 – Triangle Shirtwaist Factory Fire Kills 146 in New York City

On March 25th, 1911, one of the deadliest industrial disasters in American history occurred when a fire broke out at the Triangle Shirtwaist Factory in New York City. In just 18 minutes, 146 garment workers—most of them young immigrant women—lost their lives.

The fire started on the eighth floor of the Asch Building and quickly spread. Workers found exits locked or blocked, a common but illegal practice to prevent theft and unscheduled breaks. With no safe escape, many jumped to their deaths from the upper floors while onlookers watched in horror.

The tragedy shocked the nation and led to public outrage. It became a catalyst for the American labor movement and brought about significant reforms in workplace safety, fire codes, and workers' rights.

Frances Perkins, who witnessed the fire and later became the first female U.S. Secretary of Labor, called it the day the New Deal began. The Triangle fire remains a haunting reminder of the cost of unchecked industrial greed.

March 26th

1979 – Egypt and Israel Sign Peace Treaty in Washington, D.C.

On March 26th, 1979, Egyptian President Anwar Sadat and Israeli Prime Minister Menachem Begin signed a historic peace treaty at the White House, with U.S. President Jimmy Carter presiding. It was the first peace agreement between Israel and an Arab country.

The treaty followed the 1978 Camp David Accords and ended three decades of hostilities between the two nations. Egypt became the first Arab country to officially recognise Israel, while Israel agreed to withdraw from the Sinai Peninsula, which it had occupied since the Six-Day War in 1967.

The deal was controversial in both countries. Sadat faced condemnation from other Arab leaders and was later assassinated in 1981 by extremists opposed to the peace agreement. Begin also encountered fierce opposition at home.

Despite the challenges, the Egypt-Israel treaty has endured, remaining a cornerstone of Middle Eastern diplomacy. It demonstrated that negotiation and compromise could replace war in one of the world's most volatile regions.

March 27th

1998 – U.S. FDA Approves Viagra for Use in Treating Erectile Dysfunction

On March 27th, 1998, the U.S. Food and Drug Administration approved sildenafil citrate, better known as Viagra, as a treatment for erectile dysfunction. It was the first oral medication of its kind and quickly became a cultural phenomenon and commercial success.

Originally developed by Pfizer to treat high blood pressure and angina, the drug's unexpected side effect during trials—improved blood flow to the penis—redirected its purpose. The blue pill revolutionised treatment for sexual health issues, removing stigma and encouraging open discussion.

Sales soared, and Viagra became one of the most prescribed medications in the world. It also inspired a wave of similar drugs and massive pharmaceutical investment in sexual medicine.

Beyond its medical use, Viagra had a broader impact on aging, masculinity, and how society discusses sexual wellbeing. It remains a key moment in both medical innovation and modern marketing.

March 28th

1979 – Nuclear Accident Occurs at Three Mile Island, Pennsylvania

On March 28th, 1979, the most serious accident in U.S. commercial nuclear power history occurred at the Three Mile Island plant near Harrisburg, Pennsylvania. A partial meltdown in Reactor 2 resulted in a release of radioactive gas and raised widespread fears about nuclear safety.

The incident began with a mechanical failure and was compounded by human error and inadequate training. Although the reactor core was severely damaged, the containment structure prevented a catastrophic release, and no immediate injuries were reported.

Nevertheless, the psychological impact was immense. News of the event spread rapidly, causing panic and leading to the evacuation of thousands. The accident eroded public trust in nuclear energy and effectively stalled new nuclear power projects in the United States for decades.

Investigations led to sweeping changes in safety protocols, training standards, and regulatory oversight. The Three Mile Island incident remains a defining moment in the debate over nuclear energy and risk management.

March 29th

1974 – Terracotta Army Discovered in Xi'an, China

On March 29th, 1974, Chinese farmers digging a well near Xi'an in Shaanxi Province uncovered fragments of what would become one of the greatest archaeological discoveries of the 20th century—the Terracotta Army.

The life-sized statues were created over 2,000 years ago to guard the tomb of Qin Shi Huang, the first Emperor of China. Thousands of intricately detailed warriors, horses, and chariots were found, each unique in appearance and expression.

The tomb itself had been known to historians, but the scale and artistry of the Terracotta Army were astonishing. It revealed insights into the military practices, craftsmanship, and imperial power of ancient China.

Today, the site is a UNESCO World Heritage Site and a major tourist attraction. The discovery continues to reshape our understanding of Chinese history and the ambitions of one of its most powerful emperors.

March 30th

1981 – President Ronald Reagan Shot in Assassination Attempt

On March 30th, 1981, U.S. President Ronald Reagan was shot and seriously wounded by John Hinckley Jr. outside the Washington Hilton Hotel. The attack shocked the nation and tested the resilience of a recently inaugurated president.

Hinckley fired six shots, hitting Reagan in the chest and wounding three others, including Press Secretary James Brady, who was permanently disabled. Reagan was rushed to George Washington University Hospital and underwent surgery. His calm demeanour and humour under pressure earned public admiration.

Hinckley claimed he acted to impress actress Jodie Foster, whom he had been obsessively stalking. He was found not guilty by reason of insanity and institutionalised for decades.

The shooting led to increased security for U.S. presidents and spurred the Brady Handgun Violence Prevention Act, passed in 1993. Reagan's survival strengthened his popularity and reinforced his image as a strong and steady leader.

March 31st

1889 – Eiffel Tower Officially Opened in Paris

On March 31st, 1889, the Eiffel Tower was officially opened to the public in Paris, becoming the tallest man-made structure in the world at the time. Designed by engineer Gustave Eiffel for the 1889 Exposition Universelle, the tower symbolised modern engineering and industrial progress.

Standing 300 meters tall (984 feet), the iron tower was initially controversial. Many Parisians, including prominent artists and intellectuals, denounced it as an eyesore. Eiffel defended it as a triumph of scientific design and insisted it would become beloved in time.

They were right. Over the years, the Eiffel Tower transformed from a divisive landmark into a national treasure and international icon. It became a defining image of Paris and French ingenuity.

Today, the tower attracts millions of visitors annually and is one of the most recognisable structures in the world. It also serves as a radio transmission tower and has hosted countless cultural and historical events.

April 1st

1976 – Apple Computer Founded by Steve Jobs, Steve Wozniak, and Ronald Wayne

On April 1st, 1976, Steve Jobs, Steve Wozniak, and Ronald Wayne founded Apple Computer in Cupertino, California. What began in a garage would grow into one of the most valuable and influential technology companies in the world.

Their first product, the Apple I, was a personal computer designed and hand-built by Wozniak. Jobs handled marketing and vision, while Wayne briefly joined to manage documentation and legalities before selling his stake just days later for $800.

Apple helped revolutionise the personal computing industry with the Apple II, Macintosh, and later, devices like the iPod, iPhone, and iPad. The company became known for its sleek design, user-friendly interfaces, and innovative software.

From humble beginnings, Apple reshaped global culture and communication. Its legacy is not just in technology, but in how people live, work, and connect in the 21st century.

April 2nd

1982 – Argentina Invades the Falkland Islands, Starting the Falklands War

On April 2nd, 1982, Argentine forces invaded the Falkland Islands, a British overseas territory in the South Atlantic, triggering the Falklands War. Argentina's military junta claimed sovereignty over the islands, which it calls the Islas Malvinas, and sought to rally domestic support through the invasion.

The British government, led by Prime Minister Margaret Thatcher, responded swiftly. A naval task force was dispatched to retake the islands, and after weeks of intense fighting, British forces regained control by mid-June.

The war lasted 74 days and resulted in the deaths of 649 Argentine and 255 British personnel. Though brief, it had lasting political consequences in both countries. Argentina's defeat led to the fall of the military regime, while Thatcher's popularity surged.

The sovereignty of the islands remains a sensitive issue, but the people of the Falklands have repeatedly affirmed their desire to remain under British rule. The war is remembered for its patriotism, controversy, and the harsh realities of modern combat.

April 3rd

1973 – First Mobile Phone Call Made by Martin Cooper

On April 3rd, 1973, Motorola executive Martin Cooper made the world's first mobile phone call using a handheld device. Calling his rival at Bell Labs, Cooper introduced a new era in telecommunications while standing on a street in New York City.

The phone, a prototype known as the DynaTAC, weighed over 2 kilograms and had a battery life of just 20 minutes. But its implications were revolutionary. For the first time, a person could communicate while walking around untethered from wires or buildings.

It would take another decade before mobile phones became commercially available, and even longer before they were affordable for the average consumer. But Cooper's call marked the birth of mobile communication as we know it.

Today, billions of people use mobile phones for everything from messaging to banking to navigation. Cooper's innovation laid the foundation for the global digital age.

April 4th

1968 – Martin Luther King Jr. Assassinated in Memphis, Tennessee

On April 4th, 1968, civil rights leader Dr. Martin Luther King Jr. was assassinated while standing on the balcony of the Lorraine Motel in Memphis, Tennessee. He was 39 years old and had come to support striking sanitation workers.

King was shot by James Earl Ray, a fugitive who was later captured and sentenced to 99 years in prison. The assassination sent shockwaves across the United States and the world, sparking riots in dozens of cities and a period of deep mourning.

Dr. King had become the face of the civil rights movement through his nonviolent resistance, powerful speeches, and leadership during events like the Montgomery Bus Boycott and the March on Washington. His legacy was later honoured with a national holiday in the United States.

His death marked the end of an era but cemented his status as a martyr for justice and equality. King's message of peace and equality continues to inspire movements for human rights worldwide.

April 5th

1722 – Dutch Explorer Jacob Roggeveen Discovers Easter Island

On April 5th, 1722—Easter Sunday—Dutch explorer Jacob Roggeveen sighted a remote island in the southeastern Pacific Ocean, now known as Easter Island. He became the first known European to visit the island, which he named after the day of discovery.

Roggeveen and his crew were astonished by the giant stone statues, known as moai, that dotted the island's landscape. These statues, carved by the Rapa Nui people, stood as high as 10 meters and weighed several tons. The civilization behind them was a mystery to Europeans.

Over time, scholars have uncovered much about the Rapa Nui culture, including how the moai were transported and erected. The island became a symbol of environmental collapse and isolation, as deforestation and resource depletion contributed to societal decline long before European contact.

Today, Easter Island is part of Chile and a UNESCO World Heritage Site. The moai continue to fascinate archaeologists and tourists alike.

April 6th

1917 – United States Enters World War I

On April 6th, 1917, the United States officially declared war on Germany, entering World War I after years of neutrality. The decision marked a turning point in the conflict and in America's role on the global stage.

The declaration followed a series of provocations, including Germany's unrestricted submarine warfare, which sank American ships, and the infamous Zimmermann Telegram, in which Germany encouraged Mexico to attack the U.S. in exchange for land.

President Woodrow Wilson had campaigned on keeping the U.S. out of the war, but by April 1917, he declared that "the world must be made safe for democracy." Congress overwhelmingly approved the war resolution.

American troops began arriving in Europe in large numbers in 1918, providing critical reinforcements to the exhausted Allied forces. Their involvement helped tip the balance and bring the war to an end later that year.

The war's outcome reshaped international politics and began a new era of American influence abroad.

April 7th

1994 – Rwandan Genocide Begins After Assassination of President Habyarimana

On April 7th, 1994, the Rwandan Genocide began following the assassination of President Juvénal Habyarimana the night before. Over the next 100 days, an estimated 800,000 people, mostly from the Tutsi minority, were brutally murdered by extremist Hutu militias.

The killing was planned and systematic. Roadblocks were set up, lists of targets were distributed, and entire families were slaughtered with machetes and clubs. Neighbours turned on neighbours in one of the most horrifying genocides of the 20th century.

The international community was slow to respond. United Nations peacekeepers were present but limited in authority, and most foreign governments failed to intervene. Only after most of the killings had taken place did the world begin to act.

The genocide ended when the Tutsi-led Rwandan Patriotic Front, led by Paul Kagame, seized control of the country. Rwanda has since undergone a remarkable recovery, but the trauma remains deep. The events of 1994 are a stark reminder of what happens when hatred is left unchecked.

April 8th

1974 – Hank Aaron Breaks Babe Ruth's Home Run Record

On April 8th, 1974, Hank Aaron hit his 715th career home run, breaking Babe Ruth's long-standing record and making history in Major League Baseball. The milestone came during a game between the Atlanta Braves and the Los Angeles Dodgers in Atlanta.

Aaron had faced intense racism and death threats during his pursuit of the record. Many resented a Black man surpassing a white baseball legend, and Aaron later described the experience as one of isolation and fear.

Despite the pressure, Aaron remained focused and professional. When he sent Al Downing's pitch over the left-center fence, the stadium erupted in celebration. Two fans even ran onto the field to congratulate him as he rounded the bases.

Aaron finished his career with 755 home runs, a record that stood for more than three decades. He remains one of baseball's greatest players and a symbol of dignity, perseverance, and excellence in the face of adversity.

April 9
1865 – General Robert E. Lee surrenders at Appomattox Court House, ending the American Civil War

After four years of bloody conflict, the American Civil War effectively ended when Confederate General Robert E. Lee surrendered to Union General Ulysses S. Grant in the village of Appomattox Court House, Virginia. Lee's Army of Northern Virginia was surrounded and exhausted, and further fighting would have only led to unnecessary death. Grant offered generous terms: Confederate soldiers would not be imprisoned, officers could keep their sidearms, and soldiers could return home with their horses. The surrender marked the collapse of the Confederacy, although some fighting continued briefly in other regions. The event was handled with dignity and respect, helping to ease tensions during the fragile post-war period. April 9 became a symbolic end to the bloodiest war in U.S. history.

April 10
1912 – RMS Titanic departs Southampton on its maiden voyage

The RMS Titanic, the largest and most luxurious passenger ship of its time, set sail from Southampton, England, bound for New York. Built by the White Star Line, the ship was hailed as the pinnacle of maritime engineering. On board were more than 2,200 passengers and crew, ranging from wealthy elites in first class to immigrants in steerage hoping for a new life in America. The ship featured opulent dining rooms, a gymnasium, and even a swimming pool. Titanic was considered "unsinkable" due to its advanced safety features, yet this maiden voyage would become one of the most infamous journeys in history. Just four days later, disaster would strike in the icy North Atlantic.

April 11
1970 – Apollo 13 launches on a mission to the Moon

NASA launched Apollo 13, the third crewed mission intended to land on the Moon. The crew consisted of Commander James Lovell, Command Module Pilot Jack Swigert, and Lunar Module Pilot Fred Haise. The mission proceeded smoothly at first, but two days in, an oxygen tank exploded in the service module. The famous transmission "Houston, we've had a problem" signaled the start of a tense and dramatic effort to bring the astronauts home safely. The Moon landing was aborted, and the crew used the lunar module as a lifeboat to conserve power and oxygen. Against the odds, they safely returned to Earth on April 17. Apollo 13 became known as a "successful failure" and a testament to ingenuity and teamwork under pressure.

April 12
1961 – Yuri Gagarin becomes the first human in space

Soviet cosmonaut Yuri Gagarin made history by orbiting Earth in the Vostok 1 spacecraft, becoming the first human to travel into space. His 108-minute flight reached an altitude of over 300 kilometers and completed one orbit before safely returning to Earth. Gagarin's achievement was a major victory for the Soviet Union in the space race and captured the world's imagination. His words, "Poyekhali!" meaning "Let's go!" became iconic. Gagarin returned to Earth a global hero, and his flight opened the door to human space exploration. The mission demonstrated that humans could survive and work in space, setting the stage for future missions to the Moon and beyond.

April 13
1742 – Handel's Messiah premieres in Dublin

George Frideric Handel's oratorio *Messiah* premiered at the Musick Hall in Dublin, Ireland, to a packed audience. The piece, composed in just 24 days, told the story of Christ's life, death, and resurrection through powerful choral music and solos. Although Handel was German-born and based in London, he chose Dublin for the debut due to his popularity there and the city's vibrant music scene. The performance was a charity event, raising funds for debtors' prisons and hospitals. *Messiah* was an immediate success, and over time, it became one of the most performed and beloved pieces of Western choral music. Its famous "Hallelujah" chorus remains a highlight in classical music worldwide.

April 14
1865 – President Abraham Lincoln is shot at Ford's Theatre

While attending a play at Ford's Theatre in Washington, D.C., President Abraham Lincoln was shot in the head by Confederate sympathiser John Wilkes Booth. The assassination occurred just days after the end of the American Civil War. Booth, a well-known actor, slipped into the presidential box and fired a pistol at point-blank range. Lincoln was carried to a nearby house but never regained consciousness. He died the next morning on April 15. The assassination shocked the nation and plunged the United States into mourning. Lincoln, who had led the country through its greatest crisis and abolished slavery, became a martyr for freedom and unity. His death also set off a massive manhunt for Booth and his co-conspirators.

April 15
1912 – RMS Titanic sinks in the North Atlantic after hitting an iceberg

In the early hours of the morning, the Titanic sank beneath the icy waters of the North Atlantic, just days into its maiden voyage. The ship had struck an iceberg late on April 14, tearing a fatal gash in its hull. Despite its reputation as "unsinkable," the Titanic lacked enough lifeboats for all passengers. Of the more than 2,200 people on board, over 1,500 perished in the disaster. Many died from hypothermia in the freezing water. The tragedy shocked the world and led to sweeping changes in maritime safety laws, including requirements for lifeboats and round-the-clock radio operations. The Titanic remains a symbol of human ambition, hubris, and the fragility of life at sea.

April 16
1889 – Charlie Chaplin is born in London

Charles Spencer Chaplin, better known as Charlie Chaplin, was born in London into a family of performers. He rose from poverty to become one of the most iconic figures in cinematic history. Chaplin gained fame during the silent film era with his character "The Tramp," a lovable, bowler-hatted figure who brought humour and pathos to audiences around the world. His films, including *The Kid*, *Modern Times*, and *The Great Dictator*, combined slapstick comedy with social commentary. Chaplin's expressive acting and pioneering direction left a lasting impact on the film industry. He later moved to the United States but faced political controversy during the McCarthy era, eventually relocating to Switzerland. His influence on film and comedy remains profound.

April 17
1961 – Bay of Pigs invasion begins in Cuba

Backed by the United States, a group of Cuban exiles launched an invasion at the Bay of Pigs in an attempt to overthrow Fidel Castro's communist government. The operation, planned by the CIA under President Eisenhower and executed under President Kennedy, quickly turned into a disaster. Poor planning, inadequate support, and stronger-than-expected Cuban resistance led to the failure of the mission within days. Over 1,000 exiles were captured. The debacle embarrassed the United States on the world stage and strengthened Castro's position in Cuba. It also pushed him closer to the Soviet Union, helping to set the stage for the Cuban Missile Crisis the following year. The failed invasion remains a major lesson in the limits of covert intervention.

April 18
1906 – A massive earthquake strikes San Francisco

At 5:12 a.m., a powerful earthquake struck San Francisco, estimated at a magnitude of 7.9. The quake and resulting fires destroyed over 80 percent of the city and killed more than 3,000 people, making it one of the deadliest natural disasters in U.S. history. Buildings crumbled, gas lines ruptured, and fires raged for days. Many survivors lived in makeshift camps for months. The disaster exposed flaws in urban planning and led to new seismic building codes. The city was eventually rebuilt with a more modern infrastructure. The quake also helped advance the scientific study of earthquakes, particularly the understanding of the San Andreas Fault, which had caused the rupture.

April 19
1775 – The American Revolutionary War begins with the battles of Lexington and Concord

British troops marched from Boston to seize colonial weapons stored in Concord, Massachusetts. At Lexington, they were met by a small group of colonial militia. A shot was fired—no one knows by whom—and the American Revolutionary War began. The skirmish at Lexington was brief, but the confrontation at Concord saw the colonists fight back fiercely. As British troops retreated, they were harassed by colonial forces along the road back to Boston. The day marked the outbreak of armed conflict between Britain and its American colonies. The phrase "the shot heard round the world" was later used to describe the beginning of the struggle for American independence.

April 20
1889 – Adolf Hitler is born in Braunau am Inn, Austria

Adolf Hitler, the future dictator of Nazi Germany, was born in a small town in Austria near the German border. He would rise to power in the 1930s as leader of the National Socialist German Workers' Party, or Nazis. Hitler led Germany into World War II and orchestrated the Holocaust, in which six million Jews and millions of others were murdered. His authoritarian regime was marked by militarism, propaganda, and aggressive expansionism. Hitler's early life was marked by academic failure and a passion for art, which he pursued unsuccessfully before enlisting in World War I. His ideas would go on to reshape the world in horrific ways. His legacy remains one of the darkest in modern history.

April 21
1926 – Queen Elizabeth II is born in London

Elizabeth Alexandra Mary Windsor was born in London as the first child of the Duke and Duchess of York, later King George VI and Queen Elizabeth. When her uncle, Edward VIII, abdicated in 1936, her father became king, and Elizabeth became heir to the throne. She ascended the throne in 1952 after her father's death, beginning one of the longest reigns in British history. Queen Elizabeth II became a symbol of continuity and stability through decades of political change, international crises, and family drama. She celebrated her Platinum Jubilee in 2022, marking 70 years on the throne. Her reign defined an era for Britain and the Commonwealth.

April 22
1970 – First Earth Day is celebrated across the United States

In response to growing concerns about environmental pollution, the first Earth Day was held on April 22, 1970. It was the brainchild of Senator Gaylord Nelson and activist Denis Hayes, who organised nationwide events to raise awareness about environmental issues. Millions of Americans participated in rallies, teach-ins, and clean-up events. The movement united people from all backgrounds and political leanings. Earth Day helped lead to the creation of the Environmental Protection Agency and major legislation such as the Clean Air Act and Clean Water Act. What began as a national event has grown into a global environmental movement observed in more than 190 countries every year.

April 23
1616 – William Shakespeare dies in Stratford-upon-Avon

William Shakespeare, often regarded as the greatest playwright in history, died on this day in his hometown. His contributions to literature, language, and theatre are unparalleled. During his lifetime, he wrote 39 plays, 154 sonnets, and numerous poems. His works have been translated into every major language and are performed more often than those of any other playwright. Shakespeare captured the human experience in all its complexity, exploring themes of love, power, betrayal, and ambition. From *Hamlet* to *Romeo and Juliet*, his plays continue to influence storytelling across the world. Though little is known about his personal life, his literary legacy remains firmly intact over four centuries later.

April 24
1915 – Armenian genocide begins in the Ottoman Empire

On this day, Ottoman authorities arrested and executed hundreds of Armenian intellectuals and community leaders in Constantinople, marking the beginning of what would become the Armenian Genocide. Over the following years, an estimated 1.5 million Armenians were systematically killed through mass executions, forced marches, and starvation. The genocide was carried out under the cover of World War I and remains one of the most contested and tragic events of the 20th century. Turkey continues to dispute the use of the term "genocide," but many historians and over 30 countries officially recognise it as such. The event stands as a stark reminder of the dangers of nationalism, intolerance, and unchecked power.

April 25
1915 – ANZAC troops land at Gallipoli during World War I

In the early hours of April 25, Australian and New Zealand Army Corps (ANZAC) troops landed on the Gallipoli Peninsula in what is now Turkey. The campaign aimed to open a new front against the Ottoman Empire, an ally of Germany. However, the troops faced strong resistance, difficult terrain, and harsh conditions. The campaign dragged on for eight months, resulting in heavy casualties on both sides. Although ultimately a military failure, the Gallipoli campaign became a defining moment for Australia and New Zealand. April 25 is now commemorated as ANZAC Day, honouring the courage and sacrifice of soldiers who served in that and later conflicts.

April 26, 1986 – Chernobyl Nuclear Disaster Unleashes Catastrophic Fallout

In the early hours of April 26, 1986, Reactor 4 at the Chernobyl Nuclear Power Plant in Ukraine exploded during a late-night safety test gone awry. The resulting blast released massive amounts of radioactive material into the atmosphere, contaminating vast areas of Ukraine, Belarus, and Russia. The nearby town of Pripyat, home to plant workers and their families, was evacuated, displacing over 50,000 residents. In total, more than 300,000 people were forced to relocate.

The Soviet government's initial secrecy exacerbated the disaster's impact, delaying international awareness and response. Firefighters and plant workers, many of whom succumbed to acute radiation sickness, heroically attempted to contain the inferno. A massive concrete sarcophagus was constructed to encase the reactor, a structure that has since been replaced by a more secure containment system.

Official death tolls remain disputed; while 56 immediate deaths were reported, long-term health effects, including cancer and birth defects, have affected countless others. The Chernobyl disaster not only highlighted the potential dangers of nuclear energy but also underscored the importance of transparency and international cooperation in managing such crises.

April 27, 4977 BCE – Johannes Kepler's Hypothetical Date for the Universe's Creation

Renowned German astronomer Johannes Kepler, in his 17th-century calculations, proposed April 27, 4977 BCE, as the date of the universe's creation. Drawing from biblical chronology and astronomical observations, Kepler's estimate reflects the period's attempt to reconcile religious texts with emerging scientific understanding.

While modern cosmology, based on the Big Bang theory, estimates the universe's age at approximately 13.8 billion years, Kepler's work was instrumental in advancing the study of celestial mechanics. His laws of planetary motion laid the groundwork for Newton's theory of gravitation and revolutionized our comprehension of the solar system's dynamics.

Kepler's efforts exemplify the transitional period in scientific thought, moving from a geocentric worldview to a heliocentric model. His dedication to empirical observation and mathematical precision marked a significant shift towards the modern scientific method, influencing generations of astronomers and physicists.

April 28, 1945 – Execution of Benito Mussolini Marks the Fall of Fascist Italy

As World War II neared its conclusion, Italian dictator Benito Mussolini attempted to flee to Switzerland with his mistress, Clara Petacci. On April 27, 1945, they were captured by Italian partisans near the village of Dongo. The following day, both were executed by firing squad. Their bodies were transported to Milan and publicly displayed in Piazzale Loreto, a symbolic act of retribution for the atrocities committed under Mussolini's regime.

Mussolini's death signified the definitive end of fascist rule in Italy. His alliance with Nazi Germany had led Italy into a devastating war, resulting in immense suffering and loss. The public display of his corpse served as a stark warning against totalitarianism and a cathartic moment for a nation seeking to reclaim its democratic identity.

The fall of Mussolini paved the way for Italy's transition to a republic in 1946, marking a new chapter in its political history. The events surrounding his demise remain a potent reminder of the consequences of dictatorial rule and the resilience of democratic ideals.

April 29, 1945 – Liberation of Dachau Concentration Camp Reveals Nazi Atrocities

On April 29, 1945, American forces liberated the Dachau concentration camp, located near Munich, Germany. As the first and one of the largest Nazi concentration camps, Dachau had been operational since 1933, initially detaining political prisoners before expanding to incarcerate Jews, Roma, and other marginalized groups.

Upon liberation, U.S. troops discovered approximately 32,000 emaciated survivors and numerous train cars filled with corpses. The horrific conditions, including evidence of inhumane medical experiments and systematic torture, shocked the liberators and the world. The camp's liberation provided irrefutable proof of the Holocaust's atrocities and underscored the necessity of bringing Nazi perpetrators to justice.

The revelations at Dachau galvanized international support for human rights and led to the establishment of legal precedents in prosecuting crimes against humanity. The camp now serves as a memorial and museum, educating future generations about the horrors of the Holocaust and the imperative of preventing such atrocities from recurring.

April 30, 1945 – Adolf Hitler Commits Suicide as Berlin Falls

As Soviet forces encircled Berlin, Adolf Hitler retreated to his Führerbunker beneath the Reich Chancellery. On April 30, 1945, facing imminent defeat, Hitler and his long-time companion, Eva Braun, whom he had married the previous day, took their own lives. Hitler ingested cyanide and simultaneously shot himself, while Braun consumed cyanide. Their bodies were subsequently burned, as per Hitler's instructions, to prevent their capture.

Hitler's suicide marked the collapse of the Third Reich and signalled the end of Nazi Germany's reign of terror. In the ensuing days, German forces across Europe surrendered, culminating in Victory in Europe Day on May 8. The demise of Hitler allowed for the dismantling of the Nazi regime and the prosecution of its leaders for war crimes.

The fall of Berlin and Hitler's death remain pivotal moments in world history, symbolizing the triumph of Allied forces over fascism and the beginning of a new era of reconstruction and reconciliation in Europe.

May 1, 1707 – Formation of the United Kingdom of Great Britain

On May 1, 1707, the Acts of Union came into effect, uniting the separate kingdoms of England and Scotland into a single sovereign state: the Kingdom of Great Britain. This political union was driven by mutual economic interests and the desire for stability, following years of conflict and political tension.

The unification established a single parliament at Westminster, standardized trade regulations, and created a unified currency. While the union faced opposition and sparked cultural concerns, it laid the foundation for Britain's emergence as a global power in the 18th and 19th centuries.

The formation of Great Britain marked a significant shift in the political landscape of the British Isles, influencing the nation's identity and its role on the world stage. The legacy of the 1707 union continues to shape discussions on national identity and governance within the United Kingdom today.

May 2, 2011 – Osama bin Laden Killed in U.S. Special Forces Operation

In a covert operation on May 2, 2011, U.S. Navy SEALs raided a compound in Abbottabad, Pakistan, resulting in the death of Osama bin Laden, the mastermind behind the September 11, 2001, terrorist attacks. The mission, authorized by President Barack Obama, was the culmination of years of intelligence work and marked a significant milestone in the global fight against terrorism.

Bin Laden had been the leader of al-Qaeda, orchestrating numerous attacks worldwide. His death was met with widespread relief and a sense of justice, particularly among the victims' families. However, it also raised questions about Pakistan's role in harbouring terrorists and the future of U.S. counterterrorism strategies.

The operation's success demonstrated the capabilities of U.S. special forces and intelligence agencies. It also sparked discussions on the ethical and legal implications of targeted killings and the ongoing challenges in combating extremist ideologies.

May 3, 1469 – Birth of Niccolò Machiavelli, Political Philosopher and Author

Niccolò Machiavelli was born on May 3, 1469, in Florence, Italy. A diplomat, philosopher, and writer, he is best known for his political treatise, "The Prince," which offers pragmatic advice on statecraft and power dynamics. Machiavelli's work departed from idealistic views of governance, emphasizing realpolitik and the often harsh realities of political leadership.

His writings have profoundly influenced political theory, introducing the concept that the ends can justify the means in governance. The term "Machiavellian" has since become synonymous with cunning and strategic manipulation in politics.

Machiavelli's legacy endures in modern political discourse, with his insights remaining relevant in discussions about leadership, ethics, and the complexities of power. His work continues to be studied and debated, reflecting the enduring impact of his ideas on political thought.

May 4, 1979 – Margaret Thatcher Becomes First Female British Prime Minister

On May 4, 1979, Margaret Thatcher made history by becoming the first woman to serve as Prime Minister of the United Kingdom. Leading the Conservative Party, she defeated Labour Prime Minister James Callaghan in a landslide general election. Thatcher's rise came during a time of economic turmoil, industrial unrest, and widespread public dissatisfaction with government.

Nicknamed "The Iron Lady" for her firm stance against the Soviet Union and her unyielding political style, Thatcher quickly implemented a wave of economic reforms. Her policies focused on reducing the power of trade unions, promoting individual enterprise, and privatising national industries. While supporters credited her with revitalising the British economy, critics accused her of widening social inequality and damaging public services.

Thatcher's premiership lasted over eleven years, making her the longest-serving British Prime Minister of the 20th century. Her leadership reshaped British politics and left a lasting global legacy. Whether admired or criticised, her impact remains undeniable.

May 5, 1821 – Napoleon Bonaparte Dies in Exile on Saint Helena

On May 5, 1821, Napoleon Bonaparte died in exile on the remote island of Saint Helena in the South Atlantic Ocean. Once the Emperor of France and conqueror of much of Europe, Napoleon had been exiled there by the British after his defeat at the Battle of Waterloo in 1815.

Napoleon spent the last six years of his life under strict supervision in a damp and windswept home called Longwood House. His health declined steadily, likely due to stomach cancer, though some theories have speculated about possible poisoning. His final words were reportedly, "France, the army, head of the army, Joséphine."

Napoleon's death marked the end of one of the most extraordinary lives in European history. Rising from humble beginnings in Corsica, he became a military genius and political reformer whose legal and administrative ideas influenced countries far beyond France. His legacy continues to inspire debate, seen either as a tyrant or a brilliant strategist who reshaped the modern world.

May 6, 1954 – Roger Bannister Breaks the Four-Minute Mile Barrier

On May 6, 1954, British medical student Roger Bannister achieved what many believed was physically impossible: he ran a mile in under four minutes. Clocking in at 3 minutes and 59.4 seconds at the Iffley Road Track in Oxford, England, Bannister became the first person to break the elusive four-minute barrier.

The record-breaking run occurred under less-than-ideal conditions, with strong winds and chilly temperatures. Bannister, paced by fellow runners Chris Brasher and Chris Chataway, made a strong final sprint to cross the finish line and make history.

Bannister's achievement was more than a personal victory — it was a psychological breakthrough. For years, the four-minute mile had seemed like a wall that human physiology could not overcome. Within weeks of Bannister's success, others began to break the barrier too, proving that mental limits are often just as important as physical ones.

Outside the track, Bannister went on to have a distinguished career as a neurologist. His triumph remains one of the most iconic moments in sports history.

May 7, 1915 – RMS Lusitania Sunk by German U-Boat

On May 7, 1915, the British ocean liner RMS *Lusitania* was torpedoed and sunk by a German U-boat off the coast of Ireland. Of the 1,959 people on board, 1,198 lost their lives, including 128 Americans. The attack shocked the world and pushed public opinion in the United States closer to joining World War I.

Germany had declared the waters around the United Kingdom a war zone and warned that ships could be targeted, but the *Lusitania* was a civilian passenger vessel. The German submarine U-20 struck the liner with a single torpedo, which caused a secondary explosion and sank the ship in just 18 minutes.

The incident sparked international outrage. Germany claimed the ship had been carrying military supplies, which the British government denied, though later evidence confirmed some munitions were on board.

While the U.S. didn't enter the war until 1917, the sinking of the *Lusitania* played a key role in turning American opinion against Germany. It remains one of the most infamous maritime disasters of the 20th century.

May 8, 1945 – Victory in Europe Day Celebrates Nazi Germany's Surrender

On May 8, 1945, the Allies celebrated Victory in Europe Day (V-E Day), marking Nazi Germany's unconditional surrender and the end of World War II in Europe. After six years of devastating conflict that claimed tens of millions of lives, the war in Europe was finally over.

The surrender was signed in Reims, France, the previous day and ratified on May 8 in Berlin. Adolf Hitler had already committed suicide on April 30, leaving Admiral Karl Dönitz to oversee Germany's final surrender. Celebrations erupted across the Allied nations. In London, King George VI and Prime Minister Winston Churchill appeared on the balcony of Buckingham Palace, greeted by cheering crowds. In New York, Times Square overflowed with people waving flags and hugging strangers.

Though the war continued in the Pacific for several more months, V-E Day was a moment of immense relief and reflection. For many, it symbolised not only the defeat of tyranny but also the beginning of a long process of rebuilding and healing across Europe.

May 9, 1950 – The Schuman Declaration Lays Groundwork for the European Union

On May 9, 1950, French Foreign Minister Robert Schuman proposed a revolutionary plan to prevent future conflict in Europe. Known as the Schuman Declaration, it called for the pooling of French and German coal and steel production under a single authority. This economic cooperation would bind the two nations, historically rivals, in mutual interest.

The proposal laid the foundation for the European Coal and Steel Community, the first of several institutions that eventually evolved into the European Union. Schuman's idea was that economic unity would make war not only unthinkable but materially impossible.

The plan was quickly supported by West Germany, Italy, Belgium, the Netherlands, and Luxembourg. It represented a bold step towards European integration, built on the idea of shared sovereignty and lasting peace.

Today, May 9 is celebrated as Europe Day across the EU, a symbol of unity and reconciliation on a continent once torn apart by war.

May 10, 1994 – Nelson Mandela Inaugurated as South Africa's First Black President

On May 10, 1994, Nelson Mandela was inaugurated as President of South Africa, becoming the country's first Black head of state. His election marked the end of decades of brutal apartheid rule and the beginning of a new era of democracy and reconciliation.

Mandela had spent 27 years in prison for his role in resisting apartheid, a system of institutionalised racial segregation. Upon his release in 1990, he led negotiations that resulted in the peaceful dismantling of apartheid and South Africa's first multiracial elections.

Held in Pretoria, Mandela's inauguration was attended by global leaders and watched by millions around the world. In his speech, he declared, "Never, never and never again shall it be that this beautiful land will again experience the oppression of one by another."

Mandela's presidency focused on healing the wounds of the past. Though challenges remained, his leadership transformed South Africa's image and inspired people around the globe with his commitment to peace, forgiveness, and equality.

May 11, 330 – Constantinople Declared the New Capital of the Roman Empire

On May 11, 330 AD, Roman Emperor Constantine the Great officially dedicated Byzantium as the new capital of the Roman Empire, renaming it Constantinople. The city, strategically located on the Bosporus Strait, was chosen for its defensible position and proximity to vital trade routes between Europe and Asia.

Constantinople would go on to become one of the most important cities in the world, serving as the heart of the Eastern Roman Empire (Byzantine Empire) for over a thousand years. It was a centre of art, culture, and Christian theology, housing architectural marvels like the Hagia Sophia.

The establishment of Constantinople marked a significant shift in imperial power from Rome to the East. It also helped preserve Roman traditions long after the Western Roman Empire fell in the 5th century.

Today, the city is known as Istanbul, but its legacy as a cultural and historical crossroads endures. Constantine's decision shaped the future of two continents.

May 12, 1937 – Coronation of King George VI After Edward VIII's Abdication

On May 12, 1937, King George VI was crowned in Westminster Abbey following the abdication of his brother, Edward VIII. Edward had caused a constitutional crisis by choosing to marry Wallis Simpson, an American divorcée, which the British establishment deemed unacceptable. Faced with public and political opposition, Edward stepped down, making George unexpectedly king.

George VI, originally Prince Albert, took the regnal name George to symbolise continuity and stability. He was thrust into leadership during a period of growing global tension that would soon lead to World War II.

Despite a stammer that made public speaking difficult, George became a symbol of resilience during the war. His determination to stay in London during the Blitz, alongside Queen Elizabeth, earned him respect from the British people.

His reign restored public confidence in the monarchy and helped steer Britain through one of its darkest periods. George VI remained on the throne until his death in 1952, after which his daughter, Elizabeth II, became queen.

May 13, 1981 – Pope John Paul II Survives Assassination Attempt

On May 13, 1981, Pope John Paul II was shot and critically wounded in St. Peter's Square in Vatican City. The attacker, Mehmet Ali Ağca, a Turkish gunman, fired four bullets into the pontiff as he greeted a crowd. Two bullets hit the pope in the abdomen, narrowly missing vital organs.

The pope was rushed to the hospital and underwent emergency surgery. Despite the severity of his injuries, he survived and made a full recovery. Astonishingly, John Paul II later visited Ağca in prison and forgave him in person — a gesture that stunned the world and exemplified his commitment to peace and reconciliation.

The motive behind the attack remains debated. Some theories suggest Soviet involvement due to the pope's support of Poland's Solidarity movement, while others link it to Ağca's affiliation with the far-right Grey Wolves group.

The event only strengthened the pope's global influence. He continued his papacy with even greater resolve, playing a key role in the eventual collapse of communism in Eastern Europe.

May 14, 1944 – German Officers Plot to Assassinate Adolf Hitler

On May 14, 1944, a group of high-ranking German military officers, including General Erwin Rommel, General Hans Speidel, and General Carl-Heinrich von Stülpnagel, intensified their secret preparations to assassinate Adolf Hitler. The conspirators believed that Hitler's leadership was leading Germany to ruin and that removing him was the only way to end the war honourably.

Although the most famous assassination attempt would occur two months later on July 20, the groundwork was already being laid in the spring. Rommel, though not directly involved in planting bombs, supported the idea of removing Hitler and advocated for negotiating peace with the Western Allies.

The conspirators faced immense risk. Germany under Hitler was a police state where betrayal meant torture and execution. Despite this, many officers were willing to risk their lives for the chance to save their country from further destruction.

Their efforts failed, and after the July plot was uncovered, many, including Rommel, were forced to commit suicide or were executed. Though unsuccessful, their resistance showed that even within Hitler's inner circle, dissent and courage remained.

May 15, 1940 – Nylon Stockings Go on Sale for the First Time in the U.S.

On May 15, 1940, nylon stockings went on sale to the public in the United States for the first time, marking the beginning of a fashion revolution. Developed by DuPont, nylon was the world's first fully synthetic fiber, and it promised to be stronger, cheaper, and more durable than silk.

When the stockings hit the shelves, they caused a sensation. Over 4 million pairs were sold within the first few days, and women lined up outside stores to get their hands on the coveted new product. Nylon stockings quickly became a staple of women's fashion and a symbol of modernity.

However, during World War II, nylon was diverted for military use, especially for making parachutes, ropes, and tents. This led to a shortage, and "nylon riots" even broke out when supplies ran out.

After the war, nylon returned to shelves and remained a fashion essential for decades. Its success launched the age of synthetic materials and reshaped the textile industry.

May 16, 1929 – The First Academy Awards Ceremony Is Held in Hollywood

On May 16, 1929, the very first Academy Awards ceremony took place at the Hollywood Roosevelt Hotel in Los Angeles. The event, hosted by the Academy of Motion Picture Arts and Sciences, lasted just fifteen minutes and honored films from 1927 and 1928.

Unlike today's glamorous spectacles, the inaugural Oscars were a quiet dinner gathering attended by around 270 people. The winners had been announced in advance, and there were only twelve categories. The Best Picture award went to *Wings*, a silent World War I epic, while Emil Jannings won Best Actor, and Janet Gaynor won Best Actress.

The Academy Awards were created to recognize excellence in filmmaking and to elevate the status of the movie industry. Over time, the ceremony grew into one of the most anticipated and celebrated events in entertainment, watched by millions around the globe.

That modest evening in 1929 was the beginning of an enduring tradition that still shapes the careers and legacies of actors, directors, and film professionals nearly a century later.

May 17, 1954 – Brown v. Board of Education Declares Segregation Unconstitutional

On May 17, 1954, the United States Supreme Court delivered a landmark ruling in *Brown v. Board of Education of Topeka*, declaring racial segregation in public schools unconstitutional. The unanimous decision overturned the 1896 *Plessy v. Ferguson* ruling, which had allowed "separate but equal" facilities.

The Court, led by Chief Justice Earl Warren, stated that "separate educational facilities are inherently unequal." The ruling was a critical victory for the civil rights movement and laid the groundwork for desegregation across the country.

The case had been brought by Oliver Brown, a Black parent whose daughter was denied entry to a white elementary school. The NAACP Legal Defence Fund, led by Thurgood Marshall, successfully argued that segregation harmed Black children and violated the Equal Protection Clause of the 14th Amendment.

While resistance to integration was fierce, especially in the South, the decision marked a turning point. It challenged institutional racism and helped inspire further actions like the Montgomery Bus Boycott and the March on Washington.

May 18, 1980 – Mount St. Helens Erupts in Washington State

On May 18, 1980, Mount St. Helens erupted in Washington State in one of the most powerful volcanic explosions in U.S. history. The eruption was triggered by a massive landslide, the largest ever recorded, which uncorked the volcano's northern flank and released a violent lateral blast.

The eruption killed 57 people, destroyed hundreds of homes, and flattened over 200 square miles of forest. Ash clouds rose 80,000 feet into the sky and spread across several states, disrupting air traffic and turning day into night in nearby areas.

Volcanologists had detected signs of increasing activity for weeks, including earthquakes and steam venting. Despite this, the scale of the eruption stunned scientists and the public. One of the casualties was David A. Johnston, a volcanologist who was monitoring the mountain and famously radioed, "Vancouver! Vancouver! This is it!" moments before the blast.

Mount St. Helens has remained active since then, with periodic eruptions and dome-building inside the crater. The 1980 eruption dramatically advanced the study of volcanology and remains a powerful reminder of nature's raw force.

May 19, 1536 – Anne Boleyn Is Executed at the Tower of London

On May 19, 1536, Anne Boleyn, the second wife of King Henry VIII, was executed at the Tower of London after being convicted of adultery, incest, and treason. Her death marked a dramatic fall from power for the queen who had once captivated the king and helped trigger the English Reformation.

Anne's downfall came after she failed to produce a male heir, and Henry's affections shifted toward Jane Seymour. Political enemies and court intrigue played a major role in her arrest and trial. The charges were likely fabricated, and the trial was widely seen as a sham designed to clear the path for Henry's next marriage.

Anne faced her fate with dignity and composure. She was executed by a skilled French swordsman, brought in to ensure a swift and precise beheading. Her final words included a prayer for the king and a declaration of her innocence.

Anne's daughter, Elizabeth, would later become one of England's greatest monarchs. Her life and death remain a haunting chapter in Tudor history.

May 20, 1927 – Charles Lindbergh Begins First Solo Transatlantic Flight

On May 20, 1927, American aviator Charles Lindbergh took off from Roosevelt Field in New York aboard the *Spirit of St. Louis*, beginning the first solo nonstop flight across the Atlantic Ocean. The 25-year-old pilot flew alone for over 33 hours without sleep or radio contact.

Lindbergh navigated through fog, ice, and fatigue before landing safely in Paris on May 21. He was greeted by an ecstatic crowd of more than 100,000 people. His daring journey captured the world's imagination and earned him instant global fame.

The feat demonstrated the potential of long-distance air travel and earned Lindbergh the $25,000 Orteig Prize, which had been offered to the first pilot to complete such a flight. The *Spirit of St. Louis* became an enduring symbol of aviation achievement.

Lindbergh's flight marked the dawn of a new era in aviation and helped pave the way for the development of international air travel. His bravery and skill turned him into a national hero and a pioneer of modern flight.

May 21, 1881 – The American Red Cross Is Established

On May 21, 1881, Clara Barton founded the American Red Cross in Washington, D.C. Barton, who had earned national recognition as a nurse during the Civil War, was inspired by the International Red Cross movement in Europe and sought to bring its principles to the United States.

The organization's mission was to provide emergency assistance, disaster relief, and education. In its early years, the American Red Cross responded to house fires, floods, and hurricanes, as well as helping displaced families and war victims.

Under Barton's leadership, the group became a trusted and respected humanitarian force. She served as its first president until 1904 and fought tirelessly for its recognition and funding. Her advocacy helped the Red Cross secure a Congressional charter in 1900.

Today, the American Red Cross remains one of the leading humanitarian organizations in the world, providing blood donations, disaster response, and international aid. Barton's legacy continues to inspire volunteers and caregivers across the globe.

May 22, 1990 – Yemen Is Unified into a Single Country

On May 22, 1990, North Yemen and South Yemen officially united to form the Republic of Yemen. The unification ended decades of division between the two states, which had been governed separately since the British withdrawal from the south in the 1960s.

North Yemen was a traditional republic, while South Yemen had a Marxist government. Despite these differences, the leaders of both nations agreed to merge, hoping to create a more stable and prosperous future. Ali Abdullah Saleh, the president of North Yemen, became president of the new unified state.

The initial hope for peaceful integration quickly gave way to tension. Disagreements over power-sharing, economic disparities, and regional autonomy led to civil war in 1994. Although the north emerged victorious and reasserted control, deep divisions remained.

Since then, Yemen has continued to face political instability, including a devastating civil war that began in 2014. While the unification of Yemen was historic, the country's modern history has been marked by conflict and humanitarian crisis.

May 23, 1934 – Bonnie and Clyde Are Killed in an Ambush

On May 23, 1934, notorious outlaws Bonnie Parker and Clyde Barrow were ambushed and killed by law enforcement officers in Bienville Parish, Louisiana. The couple had gained national notoriety during the Great Depression for a string of armed robberies, murders, and daring getaways.

The ambush was carefully planned. Former Texas Ranger Frank Hamer and a group of officers tracked the gang for months, eventually setting a trap on a rural road. When Bonnie and Clyde approached in their stolen Ford V8, the officers opened fire, unleashing over 100 rounds. The car and its occupants were riddled with bullets.

Though glamorized in newspapers and later films, Bonnie and Clyde lived a violent and desperate life on the run. They killed multiple law enforcement officers and civilians during their spree, which began in 1932.

Their deaths marked the beginning of the end for several Depression-era gangsters. Their bullet-ridden car became a grim tourist attraction, symbolizing both the lawlessness of the era and the public's complicated fascination with outlaws.

May 24, 1844 – First Telegraph Message Sent by Samuel Morse

On May 24, 1844, Samuel Morse sent the first official telegraph message from the U.S. Capitol in Washington, D.C. to Baltimore, Maryland. The message, "What hath God wrought," was a biblical phrase chosen by Annie Ellsworth, the daughter of a government official who supported Morse's work.

This groundbreaking moment marked the birth of instant long-distance communication. Using a system of electrical pulses and Morse code, the telegraph revolutionized how people shared information. It paved the way for global communication networks and laid the foundation for technologies like the telephone and the internet.

Before the telegraph, messages took days or weeks to travel between cities. With Morse's invention, news and information could be transmitted in minutes. This had a profound impact on journalism, commerce, diplomacy, and warfare.

Samuel Morse, originally a painter, dedicated years to perfecting his invention. His work transformed the modern world and remains one of the most important developments in the history of communication.

May 25, 1977 – *Star Wars* Premieres and Changes Cinema Forever

On May 25, 1977, *Star Wars* premiered in U.S. theaters and revolutionized the film industry. Created by George Lucas, the space opera was an ambitious gamble for 20th Century Fox, but it quickly became a cultural phenomenon.

Combining science fiction, mythology, westerns, and cutting-edge special effects, *Star Wars* told the story of a young farm boy named Luke Skywalker who joins the Rebel Alliance to fight the evil Galactic Empire. The film introduced iconic characters like Darth Vader, Princess Leia, and Han Solo, and featured groundbreaking visual and sound design from Industrial Light & Magic and Ben Burtt.

Star Wars smashed box office records and became the highest-grossing film at the time. It also sparked a massive merchandising empire and reshaped Hollywood by proving that blockbuster franchises with extensive world-building could be immensely profitable.

The film launched a saga that now spans decades, multiple trilogies, spin-offs, and a devoted global fanbase. It changed how movies were marketed, distributed, and experienced, ushering in a new era of event cinema.

May 26, 1896 – Last Tsar of Russia, Nicholas II, Is Crowned

On May 26, 1896, Nicholas II was crowned Tsar of Russia in a lavish ceremony at the Kremlin's Dormition Cathedral in Moscow. His ascension marked the beginning of a turbulent reign that would end with the collapse of the Russian Empire.

The coronation was accompanied by disaster. A celebration in Khodynka Field to mark the occasion ended in tragedy when rumors of free gifts caused a stampede, killing over 1,300 people. Nicholas's decision to continue with the festivities despite the loss of life damaged his reputation early on.

Nicholas II inherited an empire strained by political unrest, economic inequality, and revolutionary pressures. Though personally devoted to his family and faith, he was ill-prepared to lead a country in crisis. His conservative policies, resistance to reform, and mishandling of events such as the Russo-Japanese War and Bloody Sunday only fueled discontent.

In 1917, amid World War I and domestic upheaval, Nicholas was forced to abdicate. He and his family were executed by Bolsheviks in 1918, ending over 300 years of Romanov rule.

May 27, 1703 – Peter the Great Founds the City of Saint Petersburg

On May 27, 1703, Tsar Peter the Great founded the city of Saint Petersburg on the banks of the Neva River in what was then Swedish-controlled territory. Built during Russia's Great Northern War against Sweden, the city was part of Peter's broader ambition to modernize and westernize his empire.

Peter envisioned the city as Russia's "window to the West." It was constructed in a swampy, inhospitable area but rapidly developed into a cultural and political centre. Thousands of serfs and forced labourers toiled in harsh conditions to build it, and many died in the process.

In 1712, Saint Petersburg replaced Moscow as the Russian capital, a status it retained until 1918. The city became known for its European-style architecture, canals, and grand palaces. It reflected Peter's desire to break with traditional Russian ways and integrate his country into the European sphere.

Despite its difficult origins, Saint Petersburg became a symbol of imperial power and enlightenment, and it remains one of Russia's most important cultural cities.

May 28, 1937 – Golden Gate Bridge Opens to the Public

On May 28, 1937, the Golden Gate Bridge opened to pedestrians in San Francisco, drawing massive crowds who eagerly walked across the striking new structure. At the time, it was the longest suspension bridge in the world, with a main span of 4,200 feet.

The bridge had taken over four years to construct and was considered a remarkable engineering achievement. Designed by chief engineer Joseph Strauss and with contributions from engineer Leon Moisseiff and architect Irving Morrow, it connected San Francisco to Marin County across the treacherous Golden Gate Strait.

Its Art Deco towers, International Orange colour, and graceful design quickly made it a global icon. The bridge's completion also significantly boosted the local economy by improving transportation and trade.

The following day, May 29, 1937, the bridge officially opened to vehicular traffic, and President Franklin D. Roosevelt pressed a telegraph key from Washington, D.C. to mark the occasion. The Golden Gate Bridge remains a beloved landmark and a symbol of American innovation and resilience.

May 29, 1953 – Hillary and Norgay Conquer Mount Everest

On May 29, 1953, Edmund Hillary of New Zealand and Tenzing Norgay, a Sherpa of Nepal, became the first people confirmed to reach the summit of Mount Everest, the highest point on Earth at 29,029 feet.

The climb was part of a British expedition led by John Hunt. The team made several attempts up the mountain before Hillary and Norgay made their successful push to the summit. Battling extreme cold, thin air, and exhaustion, they reached the top and spent about 15 minutes there, taking photos and planting flags.

News of their achievement reached Britain on June 2, the same day as Queen Elizabeth II's coronation, and it was celebrated as a moment of national pride. Hillary was knighted soon after, and Norgay received honours from both Nepal and Britain.

Their feat inspired generations of climbers and transformed the Sherpa community's role in Himalayan expeditions. Today, their climb is seen as one of the greatest achievements in the history of mountaineering.

May 30, 1431 – Joan of Arc Is Burned at the Stake

On May 30, 1431, nineteen-year-old Joan of Arc was executed by burning in the city of Rouen, France, after being convicted of heresy and witchcraft by an English-backed ecclesiastical court. Her death ended the short but extraordinary life of one of history's most iconic figures.

Joan claimed to have received divine visions instructing her to help drive the English out of France during the Hundred Years' War. At just seventeen, she persuaded Charles VII to let her lead a French army, which lifted the siege of Orléans and led to his coronation in Reims.

Captured by Burgundian allies of the English, Joan was put on trial by biased clergy determined to discredit her. The trial was unjust, with her accusers misrepresenting her testimony and condemning her based on dubious charges.

Joan was tied to a stake and burned in the marketplace, calling out the name of Jesus as she died. In 1456, she was posthumously exonerated, and in 1920, she was canonized as a saint by the Catholic Church. Joan remains a symbol of faith, courage, and resistance.

May 31, 1911 – RMS Titanic Is Launched in Belfast

On May 31, 1911, the RMS Titanic was launched from the Harland and Wolff shipyard in Belfast, Northern Ireland. This marked the ship's first introduction to water, watched by over 100,000 spectators. Though the ship would not be fully outfitted and ready for voyage until the following year, the event was a major milestone in the age of luxury ocean liners.

At 882 feet long and billed as the largest moving object ever built, the Titanic was designed to offer unmatched opulence and cutting-edge engineering. Owned by the White Star Line, it was one of three Olympic-class liners intended to dominate transatlantic travel.

Construction of the Titanic began in 1909 and employed thousands of workers. The launch went smoothly and without casualties, although 15 men would die during its overall construction.

Less than a year later, in April 1912, the Titanic would tragically sink on its maiden voyage after hitting an iceberg, resulting in the deaths of over 1,500 passengers and crew. Its launch remains a key chapter in one of the most infamous maritime stories in history.

June 1, 1792 – Kentucky Becomes the 15th State of the United States

On June 1, 1792, Kentucky officially joined the Union as the 15th state of the United States. Originally part of Virginia, the region had petitioned multiple times for statehood before finally gaining admission as an independent state.

Kentucky's entrance into the Union marked the beginning of westward expansion beyond the Appalachian Mountains. Known for its fertile land, rolling hills, and strategic river access, Kentucky quickly became a vital part of the young nation's agricultural and political development.

The new state adopted a constitution that allowed for universal white male suffrage without property requirements, a progressive step at the time. Frankfort was selected as the capital, and Isaac Shelby became the first governor.

Kentucky would later become a key border state during the Civil War, caught between Union and Confederate sympathies. Its location and cultural identity earned it a unique place in American history as both Southern and frontier.

June 2, 1953 – Queen Elizabeth II Is Crowned at Westminster Abbey

On June 2, 1953, Elizabeth Alexandra Mary Windsor was crowned Queen Elizabeth II in a grand ceremony at Westminster Abbey in London. Her coronation followed the death of her father, King George VI, more than a year earlier.

The event was historic in many ways. It was the first British coronation to be televised, watched by over 20 million people in the United Kingdom and millions more around the world. The ceremony followed centuries of tradition but was also a modern media event that helped shape the image of the monarchy for a new era.

At just 27 years old, Elizabeth took on the role of sovereign of the United Kingdom and other Commonwealth realms. Her coronation reaffirmed a sense of continuity and unity in the post-war years.

The reign that began on that day would become the longest in British history. Her coronation remains one of the most iconic events of the 20th century.

June 3, 1965 – Ed White Becomes the First American to Walk in Space

On June 3, 1965, astronaut Ed White made history by becoming the first American to walk in space. During NASA's Gemini 4 mission, White exited the spacecraft and floated freely in orbit, tethered only by a 25-foot cord.

The spacewalk, or extravehicular activity (EVA), lasted about 23 minutes. White used a handheld manoeuvring gun to control his movements, describing the experience as "the most natural feeling" and expressing reluctance to return inside.

His EVA was a crucial step in the space race against the Soviet Union, which had already launched the first human and the first spacewalk. White's achievement helped validate the feasibility of future lunar missions and marked a milestone in American space exploration.

Tragically, Ed White would later perish in the Apollo 1 fire in 1967. However, his pioneering EVA laid essential groundwork for the moon landings and future missions outside Earth's atmosphere.

June 4, 1989 – Tiananmen Square Massacre in Beijing

On June 4, 1989, Chinese government troops violently suppressed pro-democracy protests in Tiananmen Square, Beijing. For weeks, students and civilians had gathered in the square to demand political reform, freedom of speech, and an end to corruption.

In the early hours of June 4, tanks and armed soldiers moved into the square, opening fire on demonstrators and bystanders. The exact death toll remains unknown, with estimates ranging from several hundred to several thousand. The Chinese government swiftly imposed martial law and censored all media coverage.

One of the most enduring images from that day is the "Tank Man" — an anonymous individual who stood alone in front of a column of tanks, momentarily halting their advance. His identity and fate remain unknown.

The massacre drew international condemnation and led to sanctions against China. To this day, the Chinese government restricts discussion of the event, making Tiananmen Square a symbol of both resistance and repression.

June 5, 1967 – Six-Day War Begins in the Middle East

On June 5, 1967, Israel launched a surprise pre-emptive attack on Egypt, marking the beginning of the Six-Day War. Tensions between Israel and its Arab neighbours, particularly Egypt, Syria, and Jordan, had been escalating for weeks.

In a lightning military campaign, Israel destroyed much of the Egyptian Air Force on the ground, quickly gaining the upper hand. Over the following days, Israel captured the Sinai Peninsula, Gaza Strip, West Bank, and Golan Heights. By June 10, a ceasefire was declared.

The war dramatically altered the map of the Middle East. Israel's territorial gains tripled its land area and brought millions of Palestinians under its control, setting the stage for decades of conflict and negotiation.

Though Israel won a decisive military victory, the war deepened regional animosities and led to ongoing disputes over land and sovereignty that continue to shape the geopolitics of the region today.

June 6, 1944 – D-Day: Allied Forces Land in Normandy

On June 6, 1944, Allied forces launched Operation Overlord, the largest amphibious invasion in history, storming the beaches of Normandy, France. Known as D-Day, the operation marked the beginning of the liberation of Western Europe from Nazi control.

More than 156,000 troops from the United States, United Kingdom, Canada, and other Allied nations landed across five beaches: Utah, Omaha, Gold, Juno, and Sword. They faced heavily fortified German defences, rough seas, and fierce resistance.

Despite heavy casualties, especially at Omaha Beach, the Allies established a crucial foothold. Within days, they pushed inland, and within months, Paris was liberated. The success of D-Day was a turning point in World War II, signalling the beginning of the end for Nazi Germany.

D-Day is remembered for its immense bravery, coordination, and sacrifice. It demonstrated the power of international cooperation in the face of tyranny.

June 7, 1494 – Treaty of Tordesillas Divides the New World

On June 7, 1494, Spain and Portugal signed the Treaty of Tordesillas, an agreement that divided the newly discovered lands outside Europe between the two powers. The treaty was meant to resolve disputes following Christopher Columbus's voyages to the Americas.

The line of demarcation was drawn approximately 370 leagues west of the Cape Verde Islands. Lands to the west would belong to Spain, and those to the east to Portugal. This division gave Portugal control over parts of Africa, Asia, and eventually Brazil, while Spain gained most of the Americas.

Although the treaty was negotiated without input from other European powers or the indigenous peoples of the Americas, it shaped the colonial map of the world for centuries. It also laid the foundation for Portugal's claims in South America, leading to the creation of modern-day Brazil.

The Treaty of Tordesillas reveals how European imperial ambitions carved up the globe, often with little regard for the people and cultures already living there.

June 8, 793 – Viking Raid on Lindisfarne Begins the Viking Age

On June 8, 793, Viking raiders attacked the monastery of Lindisfarne on the northeast coast of England, marking the beginning of the Viking Age in European history. The monastery was a centre of learning and religious devotion, and its destruction sent shockwaves across the Christian world.

The attack was swift and brutal. Monks were killed or taken as slaves, and sacred relics were looted. Chroniclers at the time described the raid as a terrifying sign of divine punishment. The event was so significant that it was recorded in multiple contemporary sources.

The Lindisfarne raid signalled a new era of Norse expansion. Over the next centuries, Viking warriors, traders, and settlers would travel across Europe and beyond, reaching as far as North America and the Middle East.

While the Vikings are often remembered for their violence, they also contributed to trade, exploration, and cultural exchange. The events of 793 marked the start of their complex and far-reaching legacy.

June 9, 68 AD – Roman Emperor Nero Commits Suicide

On June 9, 68 AD, Roman Emperor Nero took his own life after being declared a public enemy by the Senate. His death marked the end of the Julio-Claudian dynasty and threw Rome into a period of chaos known as the Year of the Four Emperors.

Nero had once been a popular ruler, known for public performances and building projects, but over time his reign turned increasingly despotic. He executed his own mother, wife, and many senators. His lavish spending and disregard for tradition earned him enemies among Rome's elite.

When several provinces revolted and the Senate turned against him, Nero fled Rome. Realizing there was no escape, he ended his life with the help of a loyal servant. His reported final words were, "What an artist dies in me!"

With Nero's death, civil war erupted as generals vied for power. Galba seized the throne, but his rule was short-lived. The instability that followed showed the fragility of the Roman imperial system and paved the way for a new era under the Flavian dynasty.

June 10, 1944 – Oradour-sur-Glane Massacre in France

On June 10, 1944, one of the worst Nazi atrocities in Western Europe occurred in the small French village of Oradour-sur-Glane. Waffen-SS soldiers massacred 643 civilians — men, women, and children — in retaliation for French Resistance activity in the area.

The 2nd SS Panzer Division "Das Reich" was moving north to reinforce German forces after the D-Day landings. On reaching Oradour, they rounded up the villagers under the pretense of an identity check. The men were shot in barns, and the women and children were herded into the church, which was then set on fire.

Only a few villagers survived. The ruins were left untouched as a memorial on the orders of Charles de Gaulle. Today, the preserved site stands as a haunting reminder of the brutality of occupation and the cost of war.

Despite postwar trials, many of those responsible never faced justice. The massacre of Oradour-sur-Glane remains a symbol of Nazi terror in France and a deeply emotional chapter in the nation's history.

June 11, 1509 – King Henry VIII Marries Catherine of Aragon

On June 11, 1509, Henry VIII of England married Catherine of Aragon, the Spanish princess who had previously been married to his older brother Arthur. Their union began one of the most significant and controversial royal relationships in British history.

Catherine was the daughter of Ferdinand and Isabella of Spain. After Arthur's death, she remained in England and eventually wed Henry, who had just become king. The marriage was initially strong. Catherine was well-educated, politically astute, and deeply religious. She served as regent while Henry campaigned in France and even led a victory against a Scottish invasion at the Battle of Flodden in 1513.

However, the couple's failure to produce a surviving male heir led Henry to question the marriage. His obsession with securing the Tudor dynasty and his love for Anne Boleyn prompted him to seek an annulment. When the Pope refused, Henry broke with Rome, triggering the English Reformation.

This momentous act changed England's religious landscape and led to a cascade of marriages, divorces, and executions that defined Henry's reign. Catherine remained a beloved figure for many and maintained her dignity until her death in 1536.

June 12, 1898 – Philippines Declare Independence from Spain

On June 12, 1898, Filipino revolutionary leader Emilio Aguinaldo proclaimed the independence of the Philippines from Spanish colonial rule. The declaration took place in Kawit, Cavite, and marked a major milestone in the long struggle for Filipino self-rule.

The Philippines had been a Spanish colony for over 300 years. Inspired by global revolutionary movements and angered by years of repression, Filipinos launched several uprisings. Aguinaldo emerged as a key leader during the Philippine Revolution, which intensified during the Spanish-American War in 1898.

With American support, Filipino forces pushed the Spanish out of many regions. On June 12, Aguinaldo raised the new national flag and read the Act of Independence to a cheering crowd. However, true independence was delayed. After defeating Spain, the United States took control of the islands instead of recognizing the Philippine Republic.

This led to the Philippine-American War, a brutal and costly conflict. The Philippines would not gain full independence until July 4, 1946. Still, June 12 remains the country's official Independence Day and is celebrated as a moment of national pride and the birth of a nation's modern identity.

June 13, 1381 – Peasants' Revolt Reaches London

On June 13, 1381, thousands of English rebels led by Wat Tyler and others entered London during the Peasants' Revolt. This mass uprising was fueled by anger over high taxes, corrupt officials, and centuries of feudal oppression following the devastation of the Black Death.

The revolt began in Essex and Kent but quickly spread. The rebels entered London with surprising ease, and chaos followed. They targeted symbols of royal authority and the elite, including the execution of the Lord Chancellor and the Archbishop of Canterbury. Much of the city was looted or burned.

Young King Richard II, just 14 years old, bravely met with the rebels and made concessions, including promises to abolish serfdom. But after Tyler was killed during negotiations a few days later, royal forces crushed the revolt. The promises were revoked, and harsh reprisals followed.

Although the uprising was brutally suppressed, it left a lasting mark. It showed the power of collective resistance and led to slow but significant changes in England's social and economic structures. The Peasants' Revolt is seen today as a foundational event in the history of popular protest.

June 14, 1777 – The Stars and Stripes Is Adopted by Congress

On June 14, 1777, the Continental Congress officially adopted the Stars and Stripes as the flag of the United States. The resolution stated: "That the flag of the thirteen United States be thirteen stripes, alternate red and white; that the union be thirteen stars, white in a blue field."

The new flag symbolized unity and independence during the American Revolutionary War. The 13 stripes represented the original colonies, while the 13 stars stood for a new constellation among nations. Though the exact designer is debated, legend credits seamstress Betsy Ross with sewing the first flag.

Flag Day is celebrated annually on June 14 to honour this pivotal moment. The flag has undergone many changes since 1777, with stars added for each new state. Today, the 50-star flag is one of the most recognized symbols in the world.

More than just fabric, the American flag has come to represent the nation's ideals, struggles, and identity. From battlefields to the moon landing, it has flown as a symbol of pride, sacrifice, and freedom.

June 15, 1215 – King John Signs the Magna Carta

On June 15, 1215, King John of England met with rebel barons at Runnymede and affixed his seal to the Magna Carta, a historic document that would become a foundation of constitutional government.

The Magna Carta, or "Great Charter," was a response to John's abuses of power, including heavy taxation and arbitrary justice. The barons forced him to agree to terms that limited royal authority and protected certain rights for the nobility, including due process and protection from illegal imprisonment.

Though initially a practical peace treaty, the Magna Carta evolved into a powerful symbol of liberty and the rule of law. It was reissued several times and influenced later documents such as the English Bill of Rights and the United States Constitution.

While the original version mainly protected the elite, its legacy grew over centuries to encompass broader human rights. The Magna Carta is often seen as the first step toward democracy in the English-speaking world and a key milestone in the development of civil liberties.

June 16, 1904 – Bloomsday: James Joyce's Ulysses Takes Place

On June 16, 1904, the events of James Joyce's landmark novel *Ulysses* unfold in a single day in Dublin, Ireland. This date is now celebrated as Bloomsday, named after the novel's protagonist, Leopold Bloom.

Ulysses is considered one of the greatest works of modernist literature. It follows Bloom's experiences over the course of June 16, capturing the thoughts, memories, and encounters of multiple characters in extraordinary detail. The novel parallels Homer's *Odyssey*, with Bloom as a modern-day Odysseus navigating the streets of Dublin.

Joyce chose the date as a tribute to his first outing with Nora Barnacle, who would later become his wife. Bloomsday has since become a major cultural event, especially in Dublin, where fans retrace the characters' steps, dress in Edwardian costume, and read passages aloud.

Though controversial and even banned for its explicit content, *Ulysses* is now celebrated as a literary masterpiece. Bloomsday honours not just the novel but also the richness of language, the complexity of everyday life, and the enduring power of storytelling.

June 17, 1972 – Watergate Break-In Sparks Political Scandal

On June 17, 1972, five men were arrested for breaking into the Democratic National Committee headquarters at the Watergate office complex in Washington, D.C. What seemed like a minor burglary quickly unravelled into one of the biggest political scandals in American history.

The men were linked to President Richard Nixon's re-election campaign, and investigations revealed a pattern of political espionage, sabotage, and abuse of power. Reporters Bob Woodward and Carl Bernstein of *The Washington Post* played a crucial role in uncovering the story, aided by an anonymous informant known as "Deep Throat."

As the scandal widened, Nixon's attempts to cover it up only deepened his involvement. Tapes from the White House eventually exposed his complicity. In August 1974, facing certain impeachment, Nixon became the first U.S. president to resign.

The Watergate scandal changed American politics. It led to new laws on campaign finance and government ethics, and it shook public trust in elected officials. The term "Watergate" became shorthand for corruption and cover-up at the highest levels.

June 18, 1815 – Napoleon Is Defeated at the Battle of Waterloo

On June 18, 1815, Napoleon Bonaparte suffered a decisive defeat at the Battle of Waterloo in present-day Belgium. This marked the end of his rule as Emperor of the French and the conclusion of the Napoleonic Wars that had raged across Europe for over a decade.

After escaping exile on Elba earlier that year, Napoleon returned to power for a brief period known as the Hundred Days. European powers quickly formed a coalition to stop him. At Waterloo, British forces under the Duke of Wellington, along with Prussian troops led by Gebhard von Blücher, faced off against Napoleon's army.

The battle was brutal and closely fought. Heavy rain delayed the French attack, and when the Prussians arrived in the afternoon, Napoleon's forces began to collapse. By nightfall, the French army was in full retreat.

Napoleon was exiled again, this time to the remote island of Saint Helena in the South Atlantic, where he would die in 1821. The defeat at Waterloo ended an era of warfare and reshaped Europe, ushering in a century of relative peace known as the Concert of Europe.

June 19, 1865 – Juneteenth: Slavery Ends in Texas

On June 19, 1865, Union General Gordon Granger arrived in Galveston, Texas, and issued General Order No. 3, declaring that all enslaved people in Texas were free. This came more than two years after President Abraham Lincoln had issued the Emancipation Proclamation.

Texas was the most remote of the Confederate states, and the lack of Union presence meant that slavery had continued there despite the war's end. When Granger and his troops arrived, they enforced emancipation, bringing freedom to approximately 250,000 people.

This day became known as "Juneteenth," a blend of "June" and "nineteenth." Celebrated annually, especially among African American communities, it marks the true end of slavery in the United States. It is a day of remembrance, reflection, and celebration of Black freedom and culture.

Juneteenth was made a federal holiday in 2021, recognizing its historical and cultural significance. It stands as a powerful reminder of the long struggle for freedom and equality in America.

June 20, 1789 – The Tennis Court Oath Is Taken

On June 20, 1789, members of the French Third Estate, representing the common people, gathered at a tennis court in Versailles and took an extraordinary oath. They pledged not to disband until they had created a new constitution for France, marking the birth of the National Assembly and the beginning of the French Revolution.

Just days earlier, King Louis XVI had locked them out of their usual meeting hall. In defiance, they moved to a nearby indoor tennis court. There, led by figures like Jean-Sylvain Bailly and Emmanuel-Joseph Sieyès, they vowed to stand united.

The Tennis Court Oath was more than symbolic. It challenged the authority of the king and the rigid structure of the Ancien Régime, where the clergy and nobility held disproportionate power. It represented a shift toward democracy and the idea that sovereignty resided with the people.

This act of unity and determination was a turning point. In the weeks that followed, revolutionary fervor spread, culminating in the storming of the Bastille on July 14. The Tennis Court Oath remains a foundational moment in the history of modern democracy.

June 21, 1948 – Columbia Records Introduces the LP Record

On June 21, 1948, Columbia Records introduced the first long-playing (LP) vinyl record at a press conference in New York City. The 12-inch, 33⅓ RPM disc revolutionized the music industry by offering up to 23 minutes of playback per side, compared to just a few minutes on earlier 78 RPM records.

The LP was developed by a team led by Peter Goldmark, who sought to improve sound quality and playing time. This innovation allowed entire albums to be recorded on a single disc, changing how people experienced music. For the first time, artists could create cohesive albums with multiple tracks, instead of relying on single releases.

The LP quickly became the standard for music distribution. It enabled the rise of concept albums, classical recordings, and longer compositions. Genres like jazz, rock, and pop all flourished in the LP era.

Though CDs and digital music would later take centre stage, the LP never fully disappeared. In recent years, vinyl has made a strong comeback, celebrated for its warmth and nostalgic appeal. The format's 1948 debut remains a milestone in audio history.

June 22, 1941 – Nazi Germany Invades the Soviet Union

On June 22, 1941, Nazi Germany launched Operation Barbarossa, a massive and unprovoked invasion of the Soviet Union. It was the largest military operation in history at the time, involving over three million Axis troops along a front that stretched nearly 2,000 miles.

Hitler had long viewed the Soviet Union as both a racial enemy and a threat to Germany's eastern ambitions. Despite a non-aggression pact signed in 1939, Germany attacked in full force, hoping for a swift victory. The invasion caught the Soviets off guard and led to devastating early losses.

However, the campaign soon bogged down. The harsh Russian winter, stretched supply lines, and fierce Soviet resistance turned the tide. Key battles like Moscow and later Stalingrad reversed Germany's momentum. Operation Barbarossa ultimately failed and marked a turning point in World War II.

The Eastern Front became the deadliest theatre of the war, with tens of millions killed. The invasion also opened the door to some of the worst atrocities of the Holocaust, as Nazi ideology targeted Jews and Slavs in the occupied territories.

June 23, 2016 – United Kingdom Votes to Leave the European Union

On June 23, 2016, the United Kingdom held a historic referendum to decide whether to remain in or leave the European Union. With over 33 million votes cast, 52 percent chose to leave, setting the stage for "Brexit" and a major shift in European and global politics.

The referendum campaign was divisive. Supporters of "Leave" argued for national sovereignty, immigration control, and independence from EU regulations. The "Remain" side warned of economic consequences and the risk of isolation. The result shocked much of the political establishment and financial markets worldwide.

Prime Minister David Cameron, who had called the vote and supported remaining in the EU, resigned the following day. The Brexit process would take years to negotiate, marked by political turmoil, multiple prime ministers, and ongoing debate over the future of the UK's relationship with Europe.

The UK officially left the European Union on January 31, 2020. The 2016 referendum fundamentally altered the political landscape of Britain and challenged the idea of European unity built since World War II.

June 24, 1509 – Henry VIII Is Crowned King of England

On June 24, 1509, Henry VIII was crowned King of England at Westminster Abbey alongside his first wife, Catherine of Aragon. His coronation marked the beginning of one of the most dramatic reigns in English history, lasting nearly 38 years.

At just 17 years old, Henry was energetic, athletic, and popular. His early reign was promising, focused on justice and the Renaissance ideals of learning and chivalry. However, his quest for a male heir would dominate his rule and reshape the country.

When the Pope refused to annul his marriage to Catherine, Henry broke with the Roman Catholic Church and established the Church of England, beginning the English Reformation. Over his lifetime, he married six times, dissolved the monasteries, and centralized royal power.

His reign transformed England politically and religiously, laying the foundation for the modern British state. Though often remembered for his tyranny and many wives, Henry VIII's rule was a turning point in English and European history.

June 25, 1950 – Korean War Begins as North Invades South

On June 25, 1950, North Korean troops crossed the 38th parallel and invaded South Korea, launching the Korean War. The surprise attack, backed by the Soviet Union and later China, aimed to unify the Korean Peninsula under a communist regime.

In response, the United Nations, led by the United States, came to South Korea's aid. The conflict quickly escalated into a full-scale war, with fierce battles, shifting front lines, and devastating casualties on both sides. Seoul changed hands several times, and entire cities were destroyed.

By 1953, after three years of stalemate, an armistice was signed at Panmunjom. However, no formal peace treaty was ever concluded. The Korean Peninsula remains divided to this day, with the Demilitarized Zone (DMZ) marking the tense border between North and South Korea.

The war claimed over two million lives and left deep scars on the region. It also set the tone for Cold War conflicts around the world. The Korean War is sometimes called the "Forgotten War," but its impact on global geopolitics and Korean society has been profound and lasting.

June 26, 1945 – United Nations Is Founded in San Francisco

On June 26, 1945, delegates from 50 countries signed the Charter of the United Nations in San Francisco, creating a new international organization dedicated to promoting peace, security, and cooperation among nations. The event came just weeks after the end of World War II in Europe and reflected a global desire to prevent future conflict.

The UN replaced the failed League of Nations, which had been unable to stop the rise of fascism or the outbreak of the war. The new organization was designed to be stronger and more effective, with a Security Council, General Assembly, and various specialized agencies.

The founding signatories pledged to uphold human rights, maintain international peace, and foster social progress. The United States, Soviet Union, United Kingdom, China, and France were given permanent seats on the Security Council, giving them a central role in global diplomacy.

Since its creation, the UN has played a key role in peacekeeping, humanitarian aid, health, education, and international law. While not without controversy or limits, its creation was a landmark moment in modern diplomacy.

June 27, 1954 – World's First Nuclear Power Station Opens in Obninsk, USSR

On June 27, 1954, the Soviet Union opened the world's first civilian nuclear power station in Obninsk, a town southwest of Moscow. Known as APS-1, the plant successfully generated electricity for the local grid, marking a pivotal moment in the history of energy production.

Obninsk's reactor was small by today's standards, producing just five megawatts of power. However, it proved that atomic energy could be harnessed not just for weapons but for peaceful purposes as well. This breakthrough ushered in the nuclear age and sparked interest in developing atomic power worldwide.

The Soviets proudly presented the plant as a symbol of scientific progress and technological leadership during the Cold War. Other countries quickly followed, beginning their own nuclear energy programs, including the United States, United Kingdom, and France.

Although nuclear energy remains controversial due to concerns over safety, waste, and weapons proliferation, it has also become a major component of many countries' energy strategies. The Obninsk plant operated until 2002, but its legacy continues as the birthplace of civilian nuclear power.

June 28, 1914 – Archduke Franz Ferdinand Assassinated in Sarajevo

On June 28, 1914, Archduke Franz Ferdinand of Austria-Hungary and his wife Sophie were assassinated in Sarajevo by Gavrilo Princip, a 19-year-old Bosnian Serb nationalist. The event triggered a chain reaction of alliances and hostilities that would ignite the First World War.

The Archduke, heir to the Austro-Hungarian throne, was visiting Bosnia to inspect military forces. Tensions were already high in the region due to nationalist movements and resentment of imperial rule. Earlier that day, a failed bombing attempt had already targeted the royal couple. Later, while traveling through the city, they encountered Princip, who fired two fatal shots.

Austria-Hungary blamed Serbia for the attack and issued an ultimatum. Within weeks, the great powers of Europe were drawn into conflict due to existing alliances. The war that followed killed millions and reshaped the global order.

June 28 remains one of the most infamous dates in modern history. The assassination in Sarajevo did not just end two lives but plunged the world into a catastrophic war that would change borders, societies, and empires forever.

June 29, 1974 – Isabel Perón Becomes President of Argentina

On June 29, 1974, Isabel Perón became the President of Argentina, making her the first woman in the world to hold the title of president as a result of a national constitutional process. She assumed power following the death of her husband, President Juan Domingo Perón.

Isabel, a former dancer, had no formal education or political experience before meeting Juan Perón in the 1950s. She became active in his political movement and, after his return from exile, served as his vice president during his third term. When he died, the presidency passed to her.

Her time in office was plagued by economic decline, political unrest, and violent clashes between leftist guerrillas and right-wing paramilitary groups. She struggled to maintain control and was eventually overthrown by a military coup in 1976.

Despite her short and controversial presidency, Isabel Perón's rise to power remains a landmark in women's political history. Her tenure also set the stage for the brutal military dictatorship that followed, one of the darkest periods in Argentine history.

June 30, 1908 – Tunguska Event Devastates Siberia

On June 30, 1908, a massive explosion occurred near the Tunguska River in Siberia, flattening around 2,000 square kilometres of forest. Though no crater was found, the blast is believed to have been caused by an asteroid or comet exploding in the atmosphere.

The explosion released energy equivalent to 10 to 15 megatons of TNT, roughly 1,000 times the power of the atomic bomb dropped on Hiroshima. Trees were scorched and flattened in a radial pattern, but there were no confirmed human casualties due to the remote location.

Scientists did not investigate the site until 1927, when a Soviet expedition documented the damage. No impact crater was discovered, supporting the theory that the object exploded mid-air at an altitude of 5 to 10 kilometres.

The Tunguska Event remains the largest known impact-related explosion in recorded history. It serves as a stark reminder of the threat posed by near-Earth objects and has inspired calls for improved asteroid monitoring and planetary defence efforts.

July 1, 1997 – United Kingdom Returns Hong Kong to China

On July 1, 1997, the United Kingdom officially handed over control of Hong Kong to the People's Republic of China, ending over 150 years of British colonial rule. The transfer marked a major moment in global geopolitics and the end of an era.

Hong Kong had become a British colony after the First Opium War in 1842. It grew into a major international financial centre, blending Eastern and Western influences. The handover was agreed in the 1984 Sino-British Joint Declaration, which promised that Hong Kong would retain its capitalist system and legal autonomy for 50 years under the principle of "one country, two systems."

The ceremony was watched by millions worldwide. Prince Charles and Prime Minister Tony Blair attended on behalf of the UK, while Chinese President Jiang Zemin represented China.

Since the handover, Hong Kong has seen periods of political unrest, especially concerning issues of democracy and autonomy. While the promise of "two systems" was meant to last until 2047, its future has become increasingly uncertain.

July 2, 1964 – U.S. Civil Rights Act Signed Into Law

On July 2, 1964, President Lyndon B. Johnson signed the Civil Rights Act into law, outlawing segregation and discrimination based on race, colour, religion, sex, or national origin. It was one of the most significant legislative victories of the American civil rights movement.

The bill had faced strong opposition in Congress, including a 60-day filibuster in the Senate. It was eventually passed with bipartisan support, thanks in large part to political pressure from civil rights leaders and public outrage over violent resistance to desegregation.

The law banned segregation in public places, enforced equal access to employment, and empowered the federal government to investigate and prosecute civil rights violations. It also laid the groundwork for future reforms, such as the Voting Rights Act of 1965.

Though the Civil Rights Act did not end racism in America, it marked a fundamental turning point in the legal and moral fabric of the country. It affirmed the principle of equality and brought the federal government into a more active role in protecting individual rights.

July 3, 1863 – Battle of Gettysburg Ends

On July 3, 1863, the Battle of Gettysburg came to a close after three days of intense fighting. It marked a decisive turning point in the American Civil War, as Union forces under General George Meade repelled the Confederate army led by General Robert E. Lee.

The final day is best known for Pickett's Charge, a massive Confederate assault on the center of the Union line. The attack was a disastrous failure, resulting in heavy casualties and forcing Lee to retreat back to Virginia. It was the closest the Confederacy came to achieving a major victory on Northern soil.

The battle claimed over 50,000 lives, making it the bloodiest in American history. Combined with the fall of Vicksburg the following day, it marked the beginning of the Confederacy's slow but steady decline.

Gettysburg became a symbol of sacrifice and unity. Four months later, President Abraham Lincoln delivered the Gettysburg Address at the battlefield, redefining the purpose of the war and reaffirming the principles of liberty and equality.

July 4, 1776 – American Independence Declared

On July 4, 1776, the Second Continental Congress adopted the Declaration of Independence, formally breaking ties with Great Britain and announcing the birth of the United States of America. Drafted primarily by Thomas Jefferson, the document outlined the colonies' grievances and asserted their right to self-government.

Though hostilities had begun over a year earlier at Lexington and Concord, this marked the political moment when the colonies united in their desire to form an independent nation. The Declaration's bold statement that "all men are created equal" became one of the most influential ideals in history.

The news spread quickly, celebrated with readings, bells, and bonfires. The British government rejected the declaration, and the war would continue for several more years, but July 4 became the symbolic date of American freedom.

Today, Independence Day is a national holiday in the United States, celebrated with fireworks, parades, and patriotic displays. The Declaration of Independence remains a powerful expression of democratic ideals and human rights.

July 5, 1946 – Bikini Introduced in Paris

On July 5, 1946, French designer Louis Réard unveiled the modern bikini at a Paris swimming pool. The revealing two-piece swimsuit shocked conservative society and marked a revolutionary shift in fashion, body image, and cultural norms.

Réard named his design after Bikini Atoll, where the United States had recently conducted nuclear tests. He believed the swimsuit would cause a similarly explosive reaction. And it did. At first, the bikini was considered scandalous. Models refused to wear it, so Réard hired a nude dancer, Micheline Bernardini, to debut the suit.

Despite early resistance, the bikini gradually gained popularity. By the 1960s, it became a staple of beachwear, especially after appearances in films and magazine covers. Stars like Brigitte Bardot and Ursula Andress helped glamorize the look.

The bikini's introduction reflected deeper changes in society, including shifts toward individual freedom, body positivity, and relaxed social codes. What began as a fashion shock has become a global icon of summer and style.

July 6, 1957 – Lennon and McCartney Meet for the First Time

On July 6, 1957, a chance meeting at a church fair in Liverpool changed music history. It was the day that 16-year-old John Lennon met 15-year-old Paul McCartney. Lennon was performing with his skiffle group, The Quarrymen, and McCartney was introduced to him by a mutual friend.

McCartney impressed Lennon with his guitar skills and knowledge of rock and roll lyrics. A few weeks later, Lennon invited him to join the band. Their creative chemistry quickly became evident, and the partnership that would form the core of The Beatles was born.

The duo went on to write hundreds of songs together, many of which became global hits and shaped the landscape of modern music. Their meeting marked the beginning of one of the most influential musical collaborations of all time.

This unassuming day at a garden fête launched a journey that led to Beatlemania, cultural revolutions, and a musical legacy that still inspires millions. The Lennon-McCartney partnership remains one of the greatest in the history of songwriting.

July 7, 2005 – London Bombings Kill 52

On July 7, 2005, four suicide bombers attacked London's public transport system during the morning rush hour, killing 52 people and injuring over 700. The coordinated attacks targeted three Underground trains and a double-decker bus.

This was the deadliest terrorist incident in Britain since the Lockerbie bombing in 1988. The bombers were British citizens motivated by extremist ideology. They detonated their devices within minutes of each other, plunging the city into chaos and fear.

Emergency services responded with great bravery, helping hundreds of injured commuters. The attacks shocked the world and brought renewed focus on domestic radicalization and urban terrorism.

In the aftermath, Londoners showed resilience, returning to work and refusing to be cowed by fear. The date, known as 7/7, became a symbol of unity and defiance. Annual memorials are held to honour the victims and remind the public of the enduring need for vigilance and peace.

July 8, 1497 – Vasco da Gama Departs for India

On July 8, 1497, Portuguese explorer Vasco da Gama set sail from Lisbon on a groundbreaking voyage to find a sea route to India. His journey would change global trade and cement Portugal's status as a maritime power.

Commanding four ships, da Gama sailed around the Cape of Good Hope and up the eastern coast of Africa. He eventually reached Calicut (modern-day Kozhikode) in India in May 1498. Though initial relations with local rulers were tense, the expedition proved that the long-sought sea route to Asia was possible.

Da Gama's voyage opened the door to direct trade with India, bypassing the overland routes controlled by Arab and Venetian merchants. This dramatically increased European access to spices, silks, and other luxury goods.

The expedition marked the beginning of the Portuguese Empire in Asia and initiated centuries of European colonial involvement in the region. Vasco da Gama's successful navigation reshaped global commerce and altered the course of world history.

July 9, 1868 – Fourteenth Amendment Ratified in the United States

On July 9, 1868, the Fourteenth Amendment to the United States Constitution was ratified, granting citizenship to all persons born or naturalized in the U.S., including formerly enslaved individuals. It guaranteed equal protection under the law, forming a key part of the Reconstruction era.

The amendment was passed in the wake of the Civil War, as the nation sought to rebuild and redefine itself. It was intended to ensure that the rights of newly freed African Americans were protected, countering discriminatory Black Codes enacted in Southern states.

Though often challenged and limited in practice, the Fourteenth Amendment became a cornerstone of civil rights jurisprudence. It played a central role in landmark Supreme Court cases, including *Brown v. Board of Education* and *Roe v. Wade*.

The amendment's broad language has allowed it to be used in a wide range of civil rights struggles, from desegregation to gender equality. It remains one of the most powerful legal tools for promoting justice and equality in the United States.

July 10, 1940 – Battle of Britain Begins

On July 10, 1940, the Battle of Britain began as Nazi Germany launched a sustained air campaign against the United Kingdom. It was the first major military campaign fought entirely in the air and marked a critical turning point in World War II.

Germany aimed to gain air superiority as a precursor to invading Britain. The Luftwaffe targeted shipping convoys, airfields, and later civilian cities. The Royal Air Force, outnumbered but determined, mounted a fierce defence.

The bravery of RAF pilots, later immortalized by Winston Churchill as "The Few," prevented Germany from achieving its goals. The battle lasted until October 1940 and ended in a strategic British victory. It was the first time Hitler's plans were successfully stopped.

The Battle of Britain proved that air power could determine the course of a war. It also boosted Allied morale and showed that the Nazis were not invincible. Britain's survival in 1940 allowed it to become a crucial base for the eventual liberation of Europe.

July 11, Skylab Falls to Earth – 1979

The United States' first space station, Skylab, came crashing down to Earth on this day in 1979. After six years orbiting the planet, the abandoned space station made its fiery re-entry, scattering debris across the Indian Ocean and remote parts of Western Australia.

Originally launched in 1973, Skylab was a milestone for NASA. It allowed astronauts to conduct long-duration missions in space, studying the effects of zero gravity on the human body and performing astronomical observations. Despite some early technical issues — including damage during launch — it hosted three successful manned missions. Once the missions ended, Skylab was left in orbit. NASA hoped to boost it to a higher orbit, but delays in the space shuttle program meant it eventually succumbed to gravity.

As pieces of the station plummeted to Earth, many feared disaster. Fortunately, most of it burned up during re-entry, and no one was hurt. In a strange twist, an Australian town fined NASA for littering — a fine that remained unpaid for decades.

July 12, The Battle of the Boyne – 1690

One of the most significant battles in Irish and British history took place on this day in 1690, when Protestant King William III defeated the deposed Catholic King James II near the River Boyne in Ireland.

The clash was about more than two monarchs; it was a decisive moment in the power struggle between Protestantism and Catholicism in the British Isles. William, who had taken the throne during the Glorious Revolution of 1688, led a mixed army of English, Dutch, and Irish Protestants. James, backed by France and Irish Catholics, hoped to reclaim his throne.

Though the fighting was not particularly brutal by the standards of the time, the outcome was hugely symbolic. James fled to France, earning the mocking nickname "Seamus a' Chaca" — James the Sh*t — from his Irish supporters. William's victory cemented Protestant dominance in Ireland for generations.

To this day, the battle is remembered by Unionists in Northern Ireland, especially during annual marches on the "Twelfth of July" — events that still stir political tensions.

July 13

Live Aid Unites the World – 1985

On this day in 1985, two massive concerts in London and Philadelphia were held simultaneously to raise money for famine relief in Ethiopia. The event became known as Live Aid — and it was unlike anything the world had ever seen.

Organized by Bob Geldof and Midge Ure, Live Aid was broadcast to over 1.5 billion people across more than 150 countries. It brought together the biggest musical acts of the time, from Queen and U2 to Madonna and Led Zeppelin. The concert raised an estimated $125 million for famine victims and became a landmark moment in the history of charity, music, and television.

Queen's performance at Wembley Stadium is often considered one of the greatest live performances in rock history. Freddie Mercury's charisma and command of the crowd turned the concert into legend. The event proved how music could transcend entertainment and become a force for global change.

Despite criticisms about how the funds were distributed, Live Aid set the stage for future benefit events and showed the world what a united cultural front could achieve.

July 14

The Storming of the Bastille – 1789

The French Revolution began in earnest on this day when Parisians stormed the Bastille, a royal fortress and prison that had become a symbol of tyranny and oppression.

Tensions had been building for years. The French monarchy, led by King Louis XVI, was deeply in debt and increasingly disconnected from the suffering of its people. As bread prices soared and anger grew, citizens demanded political reform. The Bastille held only seven prisoners at the time, but its fall was massively symbolic.

When a crowd stormed the gates and seized the fortress, it marked a turning point. Soldiers defected to the people's side, and the king was forced to acknowledge the power of the masses. The storming of the Bastille is now remembered as the birth of modern democracy in France.

Every year, France celebrates Bastille Day with parades and fireworks. It's a moment of national pride — not just for a victory, but for the belief that ordinary people can stand up to power.

July 15

Twitter is Born – 2006

It may not seem like a historic date — but on this day in 2006, the first public version of Twitter was launched, changing the way people communicate forever.

Initially created as an internal messaging tool for a podcast company, Twitter allowed users to send brief, 140-character messages called "tweets." It quickly grew into a global phenomenon, helping spark movements, share breaking news, and amplify voices around the world.

From revolutions in the Middle East to presidential announcements and celebrity feuds, Twitter became a digital public square. Its simple format made it addictive, but also controversial — a space where free expression often clashed with misinformation and harassment.

Though its influence has waxed and waned, Twitter helped redefine journalism, activism, and social interaction in the 21st century. The idea that a single sentence, posted in real-time, could sway public opinion or even shift markets — that all began with a modest launch in July 2006.

July 16

Apollo 11 Launches to the Moon – 1969

On this day in 1969, Apollo 11 lifted off from Kennedy Space Centre in Florida, beginning the historic mission that would put the first humans on the Moon.

The crew: Neil Armstrong, Buzz Aldrin, and Michael Collins were propelled into space aboard a Saturn V rocket, the most powerful ever built at the time. The launch marked the climax of the space race, a Cold War-era competition between the United States and the Soviet Union. Billions of dollars, years of research, and the hopes of a nation were invested in this single flight.

Armstrong and Aldrin would go on to walk on the Moon on July 20, while Collins remained in lunar orbit. But it all began with this dramatic ascent from Earth. Millions watched the launch on television, listening to the now-famous words: "Liftoff. We have a liftoff."

Apollo 11 wasn't just a technological triumph, but it was a moment of unity, inspiration, and sheer human audacity. It reminded the world that science, when fuelled by purpose, could achieve the seemingly impossible.

July 17

The Romanovs Are Executed – 1918

In the early hours of this day in 1918, Tsar Nicholas II of Russia, along with his wife Alexandra and their five children, were executed by Bolsheviks in a cellar in Yekaterinburg.

The Russian monarchy had already collapsed in 1917, but the family had been kept under house arrest. As civil war raged across Russia, the Bolsheviks feared the Romanovs might become rallying symbols for royalist forces. Their execution was ordered in secret and carried out with brutal efficiency.

The killings shocked the world. The family had been stripped of power, but many believed they would be exiled or imprisoned and not gunned down. Rumours of surviving Romanovs persisted for decades, feeding conspiracy theories and hoaxes, most famously the legend of Anastasia.

In later years, the remains of the family were discovered and identified through DNA testing. In 2000, the Russian Orthodox Church canonized the Romanovs as martyrs. Their deaths marked the end of centuries of imperial rule and the dawn of a violent, revolutionary new era.

July 18

Nelson Mandela is Born – 1918

One of the most revered leaders of the 20th century was born on this day in 1918 in the village of Mvezo, South Africa. Nelson Mandela would go on to become a global icon of peace, resilience, and justice.

Mandela was a key figure in the fight against apartheid which was the brutal system of racial segregation that ruled South Africa for decades. As a young lawyer, he helped lead the African National Congress and organized resistance against discriminatory laws. In 1962, he was arrested and sentenced to life imprisonment.

Mandela spent 27 years behind bars, much of it on the infamous Robben Island. When he was finally released in 1990, he emerged not bitter but determined to unite his divided country. Four years later, he became South Africa's first Black president in its first multiracial election.

Mandela's life is a testament to the power of forgiveness and leadership through example. July 18 is now celebrated worldwide as Nelson Mandela International Day, encouraging people to devote 67 minutes to helping others which was one for each year he served the public.

July 19

Great Fire of Rome Begins – 64 AD

On this day in 64 AD, a massive fire broke out in Rome and raged for over a week, destroying large parts of the city. The emperor at the time was Nero and his role in the disaster remains one of history's great debates.

The fire began in the area around the Circus Maximus. Due to narrow streets and wooden buildings, it spread quickly. By the time it was extinguished, ten of Rome's fourteen districts had been damaged, with three completely levelled.

Rumours spread that Nero had started the fire himself to clear land for a grand new palace. Some even claimed he watched the flames while playing the lyre. Historians now doubt these accounts, but the myth of "Nero fiddling while Rome burned" persists. In response to the anger, Nero blamed the Christian community, marking the beginning of their widespread persecution.

Whatever the truth, the Great Fire reshaped the city and revealed how myths can be more powerful than facts in shaping legacy.

July 20

The First Moon Landing – 1969

On this extraordinary day in 1969, Neil Armstrong stepped onto the surface of the Moon and uttered the immortal words: "That's one small step for man, one giant leap for mankind."

After four days in space aboard Apollo 11, Armstrong and Buzz Aldrin descended to the Moon in the lunar module "Eagle," leaving Michael Collins in orbit. At 10:56 PM EDT, Armstrong made history as the first human to walk on another celestial body, followed shortly by Aldrin. They spent over two hours exploring, collecting samples, and planting the American flag.

The landing fulfilled President Kennedy's ambitious goal, set in 1961, to reach the Moon before the decade was out. It wasn't just a win for the United States — it was a triumph for humanity's imagination and engineering.

Over 600 million people watched the landing live. The footprint left behind is still there, preserved in the Moon's untouched dust which was a permanent symbol of what we can achieve when we dare to reach beyond our world.

July 21

Jesse James and gang commit first train robbery — 1873

On July 21, 1873, the infamous outlaw Jesse James and his gang carried out their first train robbery near Adair, Iowa. Hidden in the darkness, they pried up a section of railroad track, causing the Chicago, Rock Island and Pacific Railroad train to derail. The engine toppled into a ditch, killing the engineer instantly.

The gang boarded the wrecked train and forced the conductor to open the safe. They stole around $3,000, a significant amount at the time. Wearing masks and carrying pistols, the robbers made their getaway into the countryside, vanishing into American folklore.

This was no random act of banditry. Jesse James and his brother Frank were former Confederate guerrillas, and many of their early crimes were seen by supporters as rebellion against Northern control. The Adair robbery marked the start of a new era in American crime, where trains, the very symbol of progress, became targets.

It also made Jesse James a household name, feared by lawmen and mythologised by the press.

July 22

The Pied Piper of Hamelin – 1376

The eerie legend of the Pied Piper comes from this date in 1376, when, according to town records, a mysterious event led to the disappearance of 130 children from Hamelin, Germany.

The tale tells of a piper dressed in brightly coloured clothing who was hired by the town to rid it of a rat infestation. When the townspeople refused to pay him, he returned and lured the children away with his music. They were never seen again.

While the details are mythical, the event may have roots in real tragedy. Historians suggest it could refer to a mass emigration, plague deaths, or even a recruitment for the Children's Crusade. The story's haunting power lies in its ambiguity and the strange entry in the town's records that notes the loss without explanation.

The legend has inspired countless retellings, from the Brothers Grimm to Robert Browning's famous poem. It remains one of Europe's most enduring folk mysteries which was a chilling reminder that history and myth are often intertwined.

July 23

Coup in Egypt Overthrows the Monarchy – 1952

On this day in 1952, a group of army officers in Egypt launched a coup d'état that would end the monarchy and reshape the nation's future.

Led by the Free Officers Movement including a young Gamal Abdel Nasser, the coup was largely bloodless. King Farouk, seen as corrupt and out of touch, was forced to abdicate and went into exile. The monarchy was officially abolished the following year.

The revolution aimed to rid Egypt of British influence, land inequality, and feudal power structures. Nasser would later emerge as the nation's leader, introducing sweeping reforms and championing Arab nationalism.

The 1952 revolution marked the birth of modern Egypt and inspired other anti-colonial movements across the Arab world and Africa. Though later marred by authoritarianism, the coup is still commemorated in Egypt as a turning point when the people, through their army, reclaimed control of their future.

July 24

Machu Picchu is rediscovered by Hiram Bingham — 1911

On July 24, 1911, American historian Hiram Bingham stumbled upon the Inca citadel of Machu Picchu in the Andes Mountains of Peru. Guided by local farmers, Bingham found the site almost completely covered in jungle vegetation, its structures largely forgotten outside the region.

Though local Quechua people had long known of the ruins, Bingham's expedition brought international attention to Machu Picchu. He believed it to be the lost city of Vilcabamba, the last refuge of the Inca, though later research showed it was a royal estate built by Emperor Pachacuti in the 15th century.

Machu Picchu's stone temples, terraces, and dramatic mountain setting amazed archaeologists and tourists alike. It quickly became one of the most iconic symbols of ancient engineering and Andean civilization.

Today, Machu Picchu is a UNESCO World Heritage Site and one of the most visited places in South America, offering a glimpse into the skill and power of the Inca Empire.

July 25

First successful Channel swim - 1875

On July 25, 1875, Englishman Matthew Webb became the first person to swim across the English Channel without artificial aids. He plunged into the water at Dover and emerged near Calais, France, nearly 22 hours later.

The 21-mile stretch between England and France is known for strong currents, cold water, and unpredictable weather. Webb battled jellyfish stings, waves, and exhaustion, but kept going with a mixture of breaststroke and sheer determination. He was coated in porpoise oil to help insulate him from the chill.

His feat captured the imagination of the Victorian public. Webb became a national hero, celebrated for his courage and endurance. His swim proved that such a crossing was possible and inspired future generations of long-distance swimmers.

Tragically, Webb died just eight years later attempting to swim through the Niagara River's treacherous whirlpool rapids. His legacy, however, lives on and his Channel swim remains one of the great milestones in endurance sports.

July 26

Fidel Castro begins the Cuban Revolution — 1953

On July 26, 1953, Fidel Castro launched a failed attack on the Moncada Barracks in Santiago de Cuba. Though the assault was a disaster, it marked the symbolic beginning of the Cuban Revolution.

Castro and about 160 rebels hoped to spark a nationwide uprising against the dictatorship of Fulgencio Batista. Poor planning and strong government resistance quickly crushed the assault. Many rebels were killed or captured, and Castro was arrested and sentenced to 15 years in prison.

At his trial, Castro delivered a powerful speech ending with the words, "History will absolve me." He was released two years later and went into exile, returning in 1956 with Che Guevara and others to continue the revolution.

Though Moncada was a failure, the date became the namesake of Castro's movement the 26th of July Movement and is still celebrated in Cuba today. It marked the first major spark in a revolution that would reshape the island and its place in world politics.

July 27

Korean War armistice is signed — 1953

After three years of brutal fighting, the Korean War came to a halt on July 27, 1953, when an armistice was signed at Panmunjom. The agreement ended active combat between North Korea, supported by China and the Soviet Union, and South Korea, backed by the United States and United Nations forces.

The war had begun in 1950 when North Korea invaded the South. It soon escalated into a global conflict involving hundreds of thousands of troops and resulting in millions of civilian and military casualties.

The armistice created the Korean Demilitarized Zone (DMZ), a heavily fortified border that still divides the Korean Peninsula. No peace treaty was ever signed, which means the two Koreas are technically still at war.

The Korean War is often called the "Forgotten War," but its consequences remain deeply felt. It shaped Cold War politics and cemented the division of Korea into two very different nations and a divide that continues to affect global diplomacy.

July 28

World War I begins — 1914

On July 28, 1914, Austria-Hungary declared war on Serbia, setting off the chain of events that would lead to World War I. The conflict began just one month after Archduke Franz Ferdinand was assassinated in Sarajevo by a Serbian nationalist.

In response, Austria issued a harsh ultimatum to Serbia. When Serbia's reply failed to meet all demands, war was declared. Within weeks, alliances pulled the major powers of Europe into the conflict. Germany backed Austria-Hungary, while Russia supported Serbia. France, Britain, and eventually many others joined in.

What started as a regional dispute escalated into a global war involving over 30 countries. It introduced trench warfare, machine guns, tanks, and chemical weapons on an unprecedented scale. By the time the armistice was signed in 1918, over 16 million people were dead.

July 28 is often seen as the day the modern world changed forever and a warning of how diplomacy can fail and how quickly destruction can spread.

July 29

Adolf Hitler becomes leader of the Nazi Party — 1921

On July 29, 1921, Adolf Hitler became chairman of the National Socialist German Workers' Party, or Nazi Party. His rise marked the beginning of a dark chapter in 20th-century history.

Hitler had joined the party just two years earlier. With his powerful oratory and aggressive nationalism, he quickly gained influence. At a party meeting in Munich, he demanded full control. The vote was unanimous. From that day forward, the Nazi Party would be shaped by his ideology and ambitions.

Under Hitler's leadership, the party grew from a fringe movement to a national force. He preached hatred of Jews, communists, and the Treaty of Versailles, blaming them for Germany's post-World War I struggles. In the years that followed, he would use propaganda, violence, and legal manipulation to gain absolute power.

Hitler's appointment in 1921 was a pivotal moment and it laid the groundwork for World War II and the Holocaust, leading to the deaths of tens of millions.

July 30

In God We Trust is adopted as U.S. motto — 1956

On July 30, 1956, President Dwight D. Eisenhower signed a law making "In God We Trust" the official motto of the United States. It replaced the earlier de facto motto, "E Pluribus Unum."

The decision came during the height of the Cold War. With the Soviet Union promoting atheism, American leaders wanted to emphasize the country's religious identity. The motto had appeared on U.S. coins since the Civil War, but this made it official and extended it to paper currency as well.

Critics argued that it blurred the line between church and state, while supporters saw it as a reaffirmation of national values. The motto continues to stir debate, especially in court cases and school policies.

Whether seen as a historical tradition or a political statement, "In God We Trust" remains one of the most visible symbols of American identity, found on every dollar bill and many public buildings across the country.

July 31

Harry Potter is born — 1980

Though fictional, Harry Potter's birthday on July 31, 1980, has become a cultural landmark, thanks to the global phenomenon sparked by J.K. Rowling's book series. The character's birthday matches the author's own, helping tie the wizarding world to real-life roots.

First introduced in 1997, Harry Potter quickly became one of the most recognizable characters in literature. The story of the orphaned boy who discovers he's a wizard and attends Hogwarts School of Witchcraft and Wizardry captured the imagination of millions.

The series has sold over 500 million copies worldwide and has been translated into more than 80 languages. It spawned a massive film franchise, merchandise empire, and even theme parks.

Though July 31 isn't a historical event in the traditional sense, it marks the birth of a character who has influenced a generation, shaped modern publishing, and sparked conversations about magic, morality, and growing up.

August 1

MTV launches — 1981

At 12:01 a.m. on August 1, 1981, MTV (Music Television) launched with the words "Ladies and gentlemen, rock and roll," followed by the first video: "Video Killed the Radio Star" by The Buggles. The new cable channel changed how the world experienced music.

MTV didn't just play songs — it created a visual culture around music. Artists like Michael Jackson, Madonna, and Prince used the platform to build their image, while music videos became essential for chart success. The network gave rise to the music video as an art form and helped launch entire genres.

In the decades that followed, MTV expanded into reality shows, pop culture coverage, and award ceremonies. Though it moved away from music videos over time, its impact on entertainment, fashion, and youth culture was massive.

MTV's launch marked a turning point in how people connected with music, transforming passive listeners into visual fans.

August 2

Iraq invades Kuwait — 1990

On August 2, 1990, Iraqi forces under Saddam Hussein invaded the neighbouring country of Kuwait. The move shocked the international community and set off a crisis that would lead to the Gulf War.

Iraq claimed Kuwait was stealing oil through slant drilling and argued that Kuwait had historically been part of Iraqi territory. However, most analysts saw the invasion as a grab for wealth and power. Kuwait's vast oil reserves and strategic location made it a valuable prize.

The United Nations quickly condemned the invasion and imposed sanctions. By January 1991, a coalition led by the United States launched Operation Desert Storm to drive Iraqi troops out. The war was swift, lasting just over a month, and ended with Kuwait's liberation.

The invasion and its aftermath reshaped Middle East politics and set the stage for future conflicts involving Iraq and the West.

August 3

Jesse Owens wins first Olympic gold in Berlin — 1936

On August 3, 1936, Jesse Owens won his first gold medal at the Berlin Olympic Games, stunning Nazi Germany and becoming a global symbol of excellence and defiance.

Owens, an African American track and field athlete, was competing in a stadium filled with Nazi propaganda. Adolf Hitler had hoped the games would showcase Aryan supremacy. Owens had other plans. He won the 100-meter dash in record time, then went on to win three more gold medals in the long jump, 200 meters, and 4x100 meter relay.

His victories were not just athletic achievements but they challenged the racist ideologies promoted by Hitler's regime. Back home, Owens still faced segregation and discrimination, but his triumphs helped lay the groundwork for future civil rights progress.

Jesse Owens remains one of the greatest Olympians of all time, and his performance in 1936 is remembered as a powerful moment of grace, courage, and human dignity.

August 4

Anne Frank is arrested — 1944

On August 4, 1944, the Secret Annex in Amsterdam, where Anne Frank and her family had been hiding for over two years, was raided by Nazi authorities. The arrest ended the young girl's chance at freedom and led to one of the most tragic stories of the Holocaust.

Anne had begun writing in her diary shortly after going into hiding. Her words captured the fears, hopes, and daily routines of a Jewish family in hiding. When the Nazis discovered them, the Franks were sent to concentration camps. Anne died in Bergen-Belsen in early 1945, just weeks before liberation.

After the war, her father Otto who was the only surviving member of the group published her diary. It became one of the most widely read books in the world, giving a human voice to the horrors of the Holocaust.

Anne Frank's arrest was the end of her life in hiding, but the beginning of her legacy as one of history's most poignant witnesses.

August 5

First electric traffic light installed — 1914

On August 5, 1914, the world's first electric traffic light was installed in Cleveland, Ohio, at the intersection of Euclid Avenue and East 105th Street. It had red and green lights and a buzzer to warn drivers when the light was about to change.

Before this invention, cities used police officers or mechanical systems to manage traffic, which often led to confusion and accidents. The new electric signal was a major breakthrough in urban planning, helping organize growing automobile traffic.

The light was based on a design by James Hoge and quickly proved successful. Other cities adopted the technology, and within a few decades, traffic signals had become standard worldwide.

It might seem ordinary today, but that first electric traffic light helped pave the way for safer and more efficient cities in the modern age.

August 6

Atomic bomb dropped on Hiroshima — 1945

On August 6, 1945, the United States dropped the first atomic bomb used in warfare on the Japanese city of Hiroshima. The bomb, nicknamed "Little Boy," exploded with a force equivalent to 15,000 tons of TNT, instantly flattening much of the city and killing tens of thousands.

By the end of the year, over 140,000 people had died from the blast, burns, and radiation sickness. Survivors, known as hibakusha, faced lifelong health issues and trauma.

The bombing was intended to force Japan's surrender and end World War II quickly. Three days later, a second bomb was dropped on Nagasaki. Japan surrendered shortly afterward, bringing the war to a close.

The bombings remain controversial to this day. Supporters argue they saved lives by avoiding a ground invasion, while critics point to the immense civilian suffering. Either way, Hiroshima marked the dawn of the nuclear age and raised urgent questions about war, morality, and humanity's power to destroy.

August 7

U.S. Congress passes Gulf of Tonkin Resolution — 1964

On August 7, 1964, the U.S. Congress passed the Gulf of Tonkin Resolution, giving President Lyndon B. Johnson broad authority to use military force in Vietnam without a formal declaration of war.

The resolution followed reports that North Vietnamese boats had attacked U.S. Navy ships in the Gulf of Tonkin. Later evidence revealed that the second of the reported attacks may never have happened. Nevertheless, the resolution passed almost unanimously.

It allowed Johnson to escalate U.S. involvement in Vietnam dramatically. Troop numbers surged, and the conflict grew into one of the most divisive wars in American history. By the end of the decade, hundreds of thousands of soldiers were deployed, and domestic protests intensified.

The Gulf of Tonkin Resolution became a symbol of unchecked executive power and led to a later push for greater congressional oversight in foreign policy decisions.

August 8

Nixon announces resignation — 1974

On August 8, 1974, President Richard Nixon addressed the nation and announced that he would resign from office the following day. He became the first and only U.S. president to resign.

The decision came in the wake of the Watergate scandal, a political crisis sparked by a break-in at the Democratic National Committee headquarters and a massive cover-up by the Nixon administration. As evidence mounted, including damning audio recordings, Nixon lost the support of Congress and faced certain impeachment.

In a televised address, Nixon said he was resigning for the good of the country. The next day, Vice President Gerald Ford was sworn in as president and later granted Nixon a full pardon.

Nixon's resignation marked a turning point in American politics. It shattered public trust in government and led to reforms aimed at increasing transparency and accountability.

Watergate remains a cautionary tale about power, secrecy, and the importance of checks and balances in democracy.

August 9

Atomic bomb dropped on Nagasaki - 1945

On August 9, 1945, the United States dropped the second atomic bomb of World War II on the Japanese city of Nagasaki. The bomb, nicknamed "Fat Man," exploded over the city at 11:02 a.m., killing at least 70,000 people by the end of the year.

Nagasaki was not the original target. Weather conditions had forced a change of plans from the primary target, Kokura. The bomb detonated over the Urakami Valley, destroying much of the city, including its Christian cathedral, one of the largest in Asia at the time.

Three days earlier, Hiroshima had suffered a similar fate. The Japanese government remained silent, but the second bombing pushed them to the brink. On August 15, Japan announced its surrender, bringing World War II to an end.

The attack on Nagasaki remains one of the most controversial acts of warfare in history. It demonstrated the terrifying power of nuclear weapons and left a legacy of destruction, debate, and remembrance that continues today.

August 10

The Louvre Museum opens to the public - 1793

On August 10, 1793, during the height of the French Revolution, the Louvre Museum officially opened its doors to the public in Paris. It was the first time a royal palace had been transformed into a national museum, making art accessible to ordinary citizens.

The building had been a royal residence for centuries. After the fall of the monarchy, revolutionaries decided to turn it into a museum to display the new nation's treasures. The original collection featured just over 500 paintings, many taken from the royal family and the church.

Over time, the museum expanded dramatically. It now houses some of the most famous artworks in the world, including the Mona Lisa, the Venus de Milo, and Liberty Leading the People.

The opening of the Louvre marked a turning point in how art was viewed and shared. It signalled that culture should belong to the people, not just the elite, and helped inspire other public museums around the world.

August 11

Berlin Wall construction begins - 1961

On August 11, 1961, East German troops began preparing for the construction of the Berlin Wall, a barrier that would divide East and West Berlin for the next 28 years. The physical building started the following day, but the preparations and planning were already underway.

The wall was built by the German Democratic Republic (East Germany) to stop the massive flow of people fleeing to West Berlin and, from there, to Western Europe. Between 1949 and 1961, over 2.5 million East Germans had escaped through Berlin, creating a crisis for the communist regime.

Once completed, the wall stretched 96 miles, fortified with guard towers, barbed wire, and minefields. Families were separated overnight, and any attempt to cross was met with deadly force.

The Berlin Wall became one of the most powerful symbols of the Cold War. Its fall in 1989 represented not just the collapse of a barrier, but the beginning of the end for communist regimes in Eastern Europe.

August 12

IBM introduces the first personal computer - 1981

On August 12, 1981, IBM released the 5150 personal computer, marking the beginning of the modern computer age. Though personal computers existed before, IBM's entry into the market brought mainstream credibility and widespread adoption.

The IBM 5150 came with an Intel 8088 processor, optional floppy drives, and the Microsoft Disk Operating System (MS-DOS). It sold for around $1,600, a steep price at the time, but significantly cheaper than most business machines.

What made the IBM PC revolutionary was its open architecture. IBM allowed other companies to develop compatible hardware and software, leading to a boom in innovation and competition. It also made Microsoft's software the industry standard.

The release of the IBM PC didn't just change computing. It helped reshape education, business, and entertainment. It set the stage for the digital age and made the idea of a computer in every home and office a realistic goal.

August 13

Mexico gains independence from Spain - 1821

On August 13, 1821, after more than a decade of war and struggle, Spanish forces surrendered Mexico City to the revolutionary army led by Agustín de Iturbide. This act effectively ended over 300 years of Spanish rule in Mexico.

The independence movement had begun in 1810 with Miguel Hidalgo's famous "Grito de Dolores," a call to arms against colonial oppression. Over the next eleven years, insurgent leaders fought a brutal and shifting war against royalist forces.

By 1821, political pressure in Spain and weakening loyalty among colonial troops allowed Iturbide to negotiate the Plan of Iguala. It promised independence, equality, and Catholicism as the foundation of the new nation.

Though Mexico's early years were politically unstable, August 13 became a milestone in the country's history. It marked the birth of an independent Mexican state and inspired liberation movements throughout Latin America.

August 14

Pakistan gains independence - 1947

At midnight on August 14, 1947, Pakistan was officially declared an independent nation, ending nearly 200 years of British colonial rule in the Indian subcontinent. The country was created as a homeland for Muslims, following the partition of British India.

Led by Muhammad Ali Jinnah and the All-India Muslim League, Pakistan's formation was the result of political negotiations and religious tensions. The division created East Pakistan (now Bangladesh) and West Pakistan, separated by over 1,000 miles of Indian territory.

Independence was a moment of celebration, but it also came with immense tragedy. The partition triggered one of the largest mass migrations in history, as millions of Hindus and Muslims crossed borders amid horrific violence. Up to a million people were killed.

Despite the chaos, Pakistan's creation was a turning point for South Asia. It shaped regional politics for decades to come and remains one of the most important and complex events in modern history.

August 15

India gains independence - 1947

Just one day after Pakistan, India became an independent nation on August 15, 1947. It was the culmination of a long, non-violent struggle led by figures such as Mahatma Gandhi, Jawaharlal Nehru, and many others who resisted British colonial rule.

The British Parliament passed the Indian Independence Act in July 1947, setting August 15 as the date for withdrawal. As the Union Jack came down and the Indian flag rose, Nehru gave his famous "Tryst with Destiny" speech, proclaiming India's arrival on the world stage.

Independence came at a cost. The subcontinent had been divided into two nations, and the partition caused deep communal strife. Millions were displaced, and violence spread across Punjab, Bengal, and beyond.

Despite this painful beginning, India's independence marked the end of one of the largest colonial empires in history. It laid the foundation for the world's largest democracy and a new era in Asian and global affairs.

August 16

Elvis Presley dies - 1977

On August 16, 1977, Elvis Presley, the "King of Rock and Roll," died at his Graceland mansion in Memphis, Tennessee, at the age of 42. His death shocked the world and left fans mourning the loss of one of music's most iconic figures.

Elvis had burst onto the music scene in the 1950s with his blend of rock, blues, and gospel. Songs like "Heartbreak Hotel," "Jailhouse Rock," and "Hound Dog" made him a household name. His charisma, style, and voice transformed the music industry.

By the 1970s, his health had declined. Years of prescription drug abuse and the pressures of fame had taken a toll. He was found unconscious in his bathroom and pronounced dead later that day.

Elvis left behind a legacy that reshaped popular culture. He sold over one billion records, starred in more than 30 films, and helped bring rock and roll into the mainstream. Graceland became a shrine, and his influence continues in music today.

August 17

Indonesia declares independence - 1945

On August 17, 1945, just days after Japan's surrender in World War II, Indonesian leaders Sukarno and Mohammad Hatta declared the independence of Indonesia from Dutch colonial rule.

The archipelago had been under Dutch control for over 300 years, interrupted only by Japanese occupation during the war. With Japan's defeat, Indonesian nationalists saw a chance to assert sovereignty before the Dutch could return.

The declaration was read from Sukarno's house in Jakarta. It sparked a four-year war of independence, as the Dutch tried to reassert control. The conflict ended in 1949, when the Netherlands formally recognized Indonesia's independence.

August 17 became Indonesia's national day and a symbol of its long struggle for self-rule. The declaration marked the start of a new chapter for Southeast Asia and one of the most significant independence movements of the 20th century.

August 18

19th Amendment ratified in the United States - 1920

On August 18, 1920, the 19th Amendment to the United States Constitution was ratified, granting women the right to vote. It was the result of more than 70 years of activism, protests, and tireless campaigning by suffragists.

Leaders such as Susan B. Anthony, Elizabeth Cady Stanton, Alice Paul, and many others had fought to expand democratic rights. Suffragists marched in the streets, lobbied Congress, and endured arrests and hunger strikes.

The final ratification came when Tennessee became the 36th state to approve the amendment, meeting the constitutional requirement. The deciding vote in the Tennessee legislature was cast by a young man whose mother had urged him to support women's rights.

The 19th Amendment transformed American democracy by doubling the electorate. It also laid the groundwork for future struggles for equality, including civil rights and gender justice movements.

August 19

Coup attempt against Gorbachev fails in the USSR - 1991

On August 19, 1991, a group of hardline Communist officials in the Soviet Union launched a coup attempt against President Mikhail Gorbachev. They were opposed to his reforms and the decentralization of power, fearing it would lead to the collapse of the Soviet state.

While Gorbachev was on holiday in Crimea, the conspirators placed him under house arrest and declared a state of emergency. Tanks rolled into Moscow, but they were met with widespread public resistance. Russian President Boris Yeltsin became a key figure, famously climbing atop a tank to rally protesters.

The coup lasted only three days. It failed due to poor planning, lack of public support, and the loyalty of the military to reformist leaders. Gorbachev returned to power, but the event had weakened him.

By the end of the year, the Soviet Union dissolved. The failed coup was one of the final blows to a crumbling superpower and marked the end of the Cold War era.

August 20

Viking 1 takes first clear photos of Mars surface - 1976

On August 20, 1976, NASA's Viking 1 spacecraft transmitted the first high-resolution, colour images of the Martian surface back to Earth. The mission was a major milestone in planetary exploration and deepened our understanding of the Red Planet.

Viking 1 had landed on Mars the previous month, on July 20, becoming the first U.S. spacecraft to successfully land and operate on the Martian surface. Its twin, Viking 2, would follow in September.

The photos revealed a desolate, rocky landscape with reddish soil and a thin atmosphere. The lander also carried instruments to search for signs of life, though none were found. The mission did, however, confirm that Mars once had water and a more Earth-like climate.

Viking 1 operated for over six years, far longer than expected. Its success laid the groundwork for future Mars missions and inspired generations of scientists, engineers, and space enthusiasts.

August 21

Nat Turner leads slave rebellion in Virginia - 1831

On August 21, 1831, Nat Turner, an enslaved preacher, led one of the most significant slave uprisings in American history. The rebellion took place in Southampton County, Virginia, and shocked the slaveholding South.

Turner believed he was chosen by God to lead his people to freedom. He and a small group of followers began their revolt by killing his enslaver and his family, then moved from plantation to plantation, gaining more recruits and killing more than 50 white people over two days.

The rebellion was quickly suppressed by local militias, and Turner went into hiding for nearly two months before being captured. He was tried, convicted, and hanged.

In the aftermath, white mobs killed around 200 Black people, many of whom had no connection to the revolt. Southern states passed harsher slave laws and increased restrictions on Black Americans. Turner's rebellion remains a powerful symbol of resistance against slavery.

August 22

King Richard III killed at Battle of Bosworth - 1485

On August 22, 1485, King Richard III of England was killed at the Battle of Bosworth Field, marking the end of the Wars of the Roses and the beginning of the Tudor dynasty. It was the last time an English king died in battle.

Richard had taken the throne in 1483 after the mysterious disappearance of his nephews, the "Princes in the Tower." His rule was short and controversial, with many seeing him as a usurper.

At Bosworth, Richard faced the forces of Henry Tudor, who had a weak but legitimate claim to the throne. During the battle, Richard made a final, desperate charge toward Henry but was killed in the fighting. His crown was found and placed on Henry's head, who became King Henry VII.

Richard's body was buried without ceremony and lost for centuries until it was discovered beneath a car park in Leicester in 2012. His defeat ended the Plantagenet line and began a new era in English history.

August 23

Molotov-Ribbentrop Pact signed - 1939

On August 23, 1939, Nazi Germany and the Soviet Union signed the Molotov-Ribbentrop Pact, a non-aggression agreement that shocked the world. Named after the foreign ministers of the two countries, it secretly included a plan to divide Eastern Europe between them.

The agreement allowed Adolf Hitler to invade Poland without fear of Soviet intervention. Just over a week later, on September 1, 1939, Germany launched its invasion, triggering World War II. The Soviet Union invaded Poland from the east on September 17.

The pact gave both powers time to strengthen their positions. However, the alliance was only temporary. In 1941, Hitler broke the agreement by launching a massive invasion of the Soviet Union.

The Molotov-Ribbentrop Pact is still widely condemned for enabling the start of the war and the division of nations. For decades, its secret protocol was denied by the Soviet government, though it had devastating consequences for the people of Eastern Europe.

August 24

Mount Vesuvius erupts and buries Pompeii - 79 AD

On August 24, 79 AD, Mount Vesuvius erupted violently, burying the Roman cities of Pompeii and Herculaneum under ash and volcanic debris. Thousands of people died, and the cities were lost for over 1,500 years.

The eruption began suddenly and lasted for more than 24 hours. Ash and pumice rained down on Pompeii, collapsing roofs and suffocating residents. In Herculaneum, deadly pyroclastic flows incinerated everything in their path. Many victims were preserved in their final moments, their bodies frozen in ash.

The Roman writer Pliny the Younger witnessed the disaster from across the Bay of Naples and recorded a detailed account, which has provided historians with a vivid description of the event.

The ruins were rediscovered in the 18th century, offering an incredible glimpse into ancient Roman life. Today, Pompeii is one of the most famous archaeological sites in the world and a stark reminder of nature's power.

August 25

Paris is liberated from Nazi control - 1944

On August 25, 1944, Allied forces entered Paris and liberated the French capital from four years of Nazi occupation. The victory was a major morale boost for the Allies and for the people of France.

After the D-Day landings in June, Allied troops moved steadily across France. Resistance fighters inside Paris began an uprising on August 19, and General Charles de Gaulle insisted that French forces should lead the final push into the city.

The German commander, General Dietrich von Choltitz, defied Hitler's orders to destroy Paris and instead surrendered the city with minimal damage. That same day, de Gaulle marched triumphantly down the Champs-Élysées and addressed the nation.

The liberation of Paris marked a turning point in the war and restored French pride. It was also a powerful symbol of resistance, unity, and the eventual defeat of fascism in Europe.

August 26

Women compete in the Olympics for the first time - 1928

On August 26, 1928, women were allowed to compete in Olympic track and field events for the first time during the Amsterdam Games. It was a major step forward for gender equality in sports.

Before 1928, women had only been allowed to participate in a few sports like tennis, golf, and archery. The inclusion of track events, such as the 100-meter dash and the 800-meter run, represented a breakthrough.

Canada's Bobbie Rosenfeld and the United States' Betty Robinson were among the standout athletes. Robinson, just 16 years old, won gold in the 100 meters, becoming the first female Olympic sprint champion.

However, the 800-meter race sparked controversy when several runners collapsed from exhaustion. Critics claimed it proved women were too weak for long distances. As a result, the event was removed from the Games until 1960.

Despite this setback, August 26 remains a landmark moment in women's sports history. It demonstrated that female athletes deserved a place on the world stage.

August 27

Krakatoa erupts with devastating force - 1883

On August 27, 1883, the volcanic island of Krakatoa in Indonesia erupted in one of the most violent natural disasters in recorded history. The explosion was heard as far away as Australia and the island of Rodrigues near Mauritius, over 3,000 miles away.

The eruption destroyed most of the island and caused massive tsunamis, some over 100 feet tall. Entire villages were wiped out along the coasts of Java and Sumatra. At least 36,000 people were killed, though some estimates suggest even higher numbers.

The blast ejected so much ash into the atmosphere that global temperatures dropped, and sunsets around the world turned brilliant red for months. The eruption even affected weather patterns and agriculture.

Krakatoa's explosion remains one of the most powerful ever witnessed. It reminded the world of nature's destructive potential and has been studied by volcanologists ever since.

August 28

Martin Luther King Jr. delivers "I Have a Dream" speech - 1963

On August 28, 1963, Dr. Martin Luther King Jr. delivered his iconic "I Have a Dream" speech during the March on Washington for Jobs and Freedom. Over 250,000 people gathered at the Lincoln Memorial to demand civil rights and economic justice for African Americans.

King's speech was the emotional climax of the march. He spoke of his dream for a nation where people would not be judged by the color of their skin but by the content of their character. His words electrified the crowd and became one of the defining moments of the civil rights movement.

The March on Washington helped build momentum for the passage of the Civil Rights Act of 1964 and the Voting Rights Act of 1965. King's speech remains one of the greatest orations in American history.

August 28 is now remembered as a day when words inspired real change and helped reshape a nation.

August 29

Hurricane Katrina hits the Gulf Coast - 2005

On August 29, 2005, Hurricane Katrina made landfall on the Gulf Coast of the United States, bringing catastrophic flooding and destruction, especially in New Orleans, Louisiana. It became one of the deadliest and most costly natural disasters in American history.

Katrina had formed over the Bahamas and strengthened rapidly. When it struck Louisiana and Mississippi, it brought 140-mile-per-hour winds and a massive storm surge. The levees in New Orleans failed, and 80 percent of the city was flooded.

More than 1,800 people died, and hundreds of thousands were displaced. The response by federal and local agencies was widely criticized for being slow and disorganized. Images of stranded residents and overwhelmed shelters shocked the world.

Katrina exposed deep flaws in emergency preparedness and highlighted long-standing racial and economic inequalities in the affected areas. It led to major changes in disaster response policies across the United States.

August 30

Thurgood Marshall confirmed to U.S. Supreme Court - 1967

On August 30, 1967, Thurgood Marshall was confirmed as the first African American justice on the United States Supreme Court. His appointment was a historic moment in the struggle for civil rights and racial equality.

Marshall had already made a name for himself as a lawyer for the NAACP, most famously arguing the landmark case *Brown v. Board of Education*, which ended racial segregation in public schools. President Lyndon B. Johnson nominated him in recognition of his achievements and leadership.

Despite resistance from some southern senators, Marshall was confirmed by a vote of 69 to 11. He went on to serve for 24 years, during which he consistently supported individual rights, civil liberties, and equal protection under the law.

Marshall's legacy continues to inspire. His life story and legal victories paved the way for future generations and proved that justice could be a powerful force for change.

August 31

Princess Diana dies in Paris car crash - 1997

On August 31, 1997, Princess Diana of Wales died in a car crash in the Pont de l'Alma tunnel in Paris. She was 36 years old. Her death shocked the world and sparked an outpouring of public grief on a scale rarely seen before.

Diana was being pursued by paparazzi when the car, driven at high speed, struck a pillar in the tunnel. Her companion, Dodi Fayed, and the driver also died. Only the bodyguard survived.

Known as "the People's Princess," Diana had become beloved for her charitable work and her open, compassionate nature. Her campaigns to raise awareness about AIDS and landmines made her a global humanitarian icon.

Her funeral on September 6 was watched by over two billion people worldwide. The tragedy also led to increased criticism of the media's treatment of public figures and calls for reform in royal protocols.

September 1

Germany invades Poland to start World War II - 1939

On September 1, 1939, Nazi Germany invaded Poland, launching the deadliest conflict in human history — World War II. The attack began at dawn with aerial bombings, artillery fire, and fast-moving tank divisions using the "blitzkrieg" or lightning war tactic.

Adolf Hitler claimed it was a defensive action, but it was a clear act of aggression. The German military quickly overwhelmed Polish forces, who were brave but outmatched. Just two days later, Britain and France declared war on Germany, keeping their promise to defend Poland and officially beginning the Second World War.

The Soviet Union invaded Poland from the east on September 17, in accordance with a secret deal made in the Molotov-Ribbentrop Pact. Poland was divided between the two powers, and its government went into exile.

This invasion marked the start of six years of global conflict that would result in over 70 million deaths and reshape the modern world.

September 2

Japan formally surrenders to end World War II - 1945

On September 2, 1945, Japan formally surrendered to the Allied Powers aboard the USS Missouri, anchored in Tokyo Bay. This event officially ended World War II, following six years of fighting across Europe, Asia, and the Pacific.

Representatives from Japan signed the surrender documents in front of top Allied leaders, including U.S. General Douglas MacArthur and Admiral Chester Nimitz. The ceremony lasted less than half an hour but marked the close of a devastating global war.

Japan's surrender came after the atomic bombings of Hiroshima and Nagasaki in early August, which killed over 200,000 people combined. Emperor Hirohito announced the surrender on August 15, but it took time to organize the formal proceedings.

World War II had claimed tens of millions of lives and left cities across Europe and Asia in ruins. The end of the war allowed for reconstruction, the formation of the United Nations, and a new world order dominated by the United States and the Soviet Union.

September 3

Britain and France declare war on Germany - 1939

On September 3, 1939, two days after Germany invaded Poland, Britain and France declared war on Germany. This marked the beginning of their involvement in World War II and confirmed that Hitler's aggression would not go unanswered.

Both countries had signed defence treaties with Poland, promising to act if it was attacked. After Hitler ignored their ultimatums to withdraw, Britain's Prime Minister Neville Chamberlain made a solemn radio announcement that the nation was at war. France followed shortly after.

The decision ended any hope of peace through negotiation. Though the early months of the war, known as the "Phoney War," involved little actual fighting in Western Europe, the conflict would soon explode across the continent.

This declaration marked a turning point in modern history. What had started as a regional invasion became a global war involving dozens of nations and millions of people.

September 4

Mark Spitz wins his 7th gold medal at Munich Olympics - 1972

On September 4, 1972, American swimmer Mark Spitz made Olympic history by winning his seventh gold medal at the Munich Summer Games. It was a record for the most golds won by an individual at a single Olympic Games — a record that would stand until 2008.

Spitz won gold in seven different events, setting world records in every single one. His victories included freestyle and butterfly races, both individual and relay. With his signature Mustache and speed, he became an international sports icon.

However, his achievement was soon overshadowed by tragedy. The very next day, Palestinian terrorists attacked the Olympic Village and took Israeli athletes' hostage, resulting in the deaths of eleven Israelis.

Despite the horror of the attack, Spitz's performance remains one of the most remarkable in Olympic history. His dominance in the pool set a new standard for athletic excellence.

September 5

Munich Olympic massacre begins - 1972

On September 5, 1972, the Munich Olympic Games were shaken by a brutal terrorist attack. Eight members of the Palestinian group Black September broke into the Olympic Village and took eleven Israeli athletes and coaches hostage.

The attackers demanded the release of over 200 Palestinian prisoners held by Israel. The crisis unfolded on live television and shocked viewers around the world. German police attempted a poorly planned rescue at a nearby airfield, which ended in disaster. All eleven Israeli hostages were killed, along with five of the terrorists and one police officer.

The Games were temporarily suspended, and a memorial ceremony was held, but the events left a permanent scar on Olympic history. It raised major concerns about security at international events.

The Munich massacre remains one of the darkest chapters in sports history. It showed that even the Olympic Games, meant to promote peace and unity, were not safe from political violence.

September 6

President McKinley is shot at Buffalo expo - 1901

On September 6, 1901, U.S. President William McKinley was shot twice by anarchist Leon Czolgosz while greeting the public at the Pan-American Exposition in Buffalo, New York. He died eight days later from infection.

McKinley had just begun his second term and was popular for leading the country through the Spanish-American War and boosting the economy. He was meeting visitors in a receiving line when Czolgosz approached with a hidden pistol and fired at close range.

Though McKinley initially seemed to recover, gangrene set in around the bullet wounds. He died on September 14, and Vice President Theodore Roosevelt was sworn in as president.

The assassination shocked the nation and led to increased security for American presidents. It also propelled Roosevelt into national leadership, setting the stage for major reforms during the Progressive Era.

September 7

The Blitz begins in London - 1940

On September 7, 1940, Nazi Germany launched a massive bombing campaign against London, beginning what became known as the Blitz. For the next eight months, the city was bombed almost every night in a brutal attempt to break British morale.

That first night, more than 300 German bombers targeted the London docks and surrounding neighbourhoods. Fires raged across the city, and hundreds were killed. Civilians took shelter in Underground stations and basements as bombs destroyed homes, schools, and landmarks.

The attacks soon spread to other cities, including Liverpool, Birmingham, and Coventry. Despite the destruction and loss of life, the British people refused to give in.

The Blitz failed to achieve its goal. British resolve held strong, and the Royal Air Force successfully defended the skies. Prime Minister Winston Churchill praised the resilience of the nation, famously declaring, "We shall never surrender."

September 8

Star Trek premieres on U.S. television - 1966

On September 8, 1966, *Star Trek* premiered on NBC, introducing viewers to the crew of the USS Enterprise and launching one of the most influential science fiction franchises of all time.

Created by Gene Roddenberry, the show imagined a future where humanity had united to explore the stars as part of the United Federation of Planets. It featured a diverse cast, including William Shatner as Captain Kirk, Leonard Nimoy as Spock, and Nichelle Nichols as Lieutenant Uhura.

The show tackled real-world issues like racism, war, and ethics through the lens of futuristic space adventures. Though it struggled with ratings and was cancelled after three seasons, *Star Trek* developed a loyal fanbase and grew into a global phenomenon through movies, spin-offs, and cultural impact.

Its vision of a better future has inspired generations of scientists, engineers, and dreamers.

September 9

North Korea is officially established - 1948

On September 9, 1948, the Democratic People's Republic of Korea (North Korea) was officially declared, with Kim Il-sung as its first premier. This marked the formal division of the Korean Peninsula after World War II.

Following Japan's defeat in 1945, Korea was split along the 38th parallel, with the Soviet Union occupying the North and the United States the South. Tensions quickly grew between the two zones. In August 1948, South Korea declared itself a republic. Just weeks later, the North did the same.

Kim Il-sung's regime was based on strict control, cult of personality, and communist ideology. In 1950, North Korea invaded the South, triggering the Korean War. The war ended in 1953 with an armistice, but no peace treaty was signed.

Since then, North Korea has remained isolated and authoritarian, ruled by three generations of the Kim family. It continues to be a central focus of global security concerns.

September 10

Elias Howe granted patent for the sewing machine - 1846

On September 10, 1846, Elias Howe was awarded a patent for a lockstitch sewing machine, a revolutionary invention that helped launch the modern textile industry. Although other inventors had worked on sewing devices before, Howe's machine was the first to use a needle with an eye near the point and a shuttle beneath the fabric — key features that set it apart.

Howe's invention dramatically sped up the process of making clothing and other goods. However, he struggled to market his idea and ended up in legal battles when other manufacturers, like Isaac Singer, used similar technology. Howe eventually won his lawsuits and received royalties, making him wealthy and cementing his place in industrial history.

The sewing machine transformed how people worked and dressed. It reduced the need for hand stitching, allowed for mass production, and made clothing more affordable. Howe's idea helped shape the rise of modern manufacturing.

September 11

Terrorist attacks strike the United States - 2001

On September 11, 2001, terrorists from the extremist group al-Qaeda hijacked four commercial airplanes in the United States and carried out coordinated suicide attacks, killing nearly 3,000 people and injuring thousands more.

Two planes crashed into the Twin Towers of New York City's World Trade Centre, causing both skyscrapers to collapse within hours. A third struck the Pentagon near Washington, D.C., and the fourth, United Flight 93, crashed into a field in Pennsylvania after passengers fought back.

The attacks shocked the world and marked the deadliest terrorist event in history. They led to massive changes in U.S. and global security, the creation of the Department of Homeland Security, and the launch of the War on Terror.

Just weeks later, U.S. forces invaded Afghanistan to dismantle al-Qaeda and remove the Taliban from power. The consequences of 9/11 are still felt today, both in international politics and in everyday life.

September 12

John F. Kennedy delivers "We choose to go to the moon" speech - 1962

On September 12, 1962, President John F. Kennedy stood before a crowd at Rice University in Houston, Texas, and delivered one of the most inspiring speeches of the 20th century. In it, he boldly declared that the United States would land a man on the Moon before the decade was out.

Kennedy's speech was a response to the growing space race with the Soviet Union, which had already launched the first satellite and man into space. The president urged Americans to rise to the challenge, saying, "We choose to go to the Moon in this decade and do the other things, not because they are easy, but because they are hard."

This speech helped rally public support and funding for NASA, leading to the successful Apollo missions and the Moon landing in 1969. It became a symbol of American ambition, innovation, and the belief in tackling the impossible.

September 13

Lawrence of Arabia dies in motorcycle crash - 1935

On September 13, 1935, T.E. Lawrence, better known as "Lawrence of Arabia," died from injuries sustained in a motorcycle crash six days earlier. A British army officer, writer, and adventurer, Lawrence had become famous for his role in the Arab Revolt during World War I.

While serving in the Middle East, he worked closely with Arab leaders to fight against the Ottoman Empire, helping to lead guerrilla raids and sabotage missions. His efforts were later glamorized in the 1962 film *Lawrence of Arabia*.

After the war, Lawrence struggled with fame and withdrew from public life. He joined the Royal Air Force under a false name and lived a quiet existence in Dorset, England. He was only 46 when he lost control of his motorcycle and suffered a fatal head injury.

Lawrence left behind a legendary reputation as a daring and complex figure in both military and literary history.

September 14

Francis Scott Key writes "The Star-Spangled Banner" - 1814

On September 14, 1814, during the War of 1812, American lawyer and poet Francis Scott Key witnessed the British bombardment of Fort McHenry in Baltimore Harbor. As dawn broke, he saw that the American flag was still flying, inspiring him to write a poem titled *Defence of Fort M'Henry*.

The poem described the resilience of American forces and the sight of the flag "still there" after the night-long attack. It was soon set to the tune of a popular British song, "To Anacreon in Heaven," and renamed *The Star-Spangled Banner*.

The song grew in popularity throughout the 19th century and was eventually declared the national anthem of the United States in 1931.

Key's words captured the spirit of a young nation fighting to defend itself. Today, the anthem is a symbol of national pride, sung at public events and sporting games across the country.

September 15

Battle of Britain reaches its climax - 1940

On September 15, 1940, the Battle of Britain reached its decisive moment when the Royal Air Force (RAF) successfully repelled a massive German air assault. The day became known as Battle of Britain Day and marked a turning point in World War II.

The Luftwaffe had launched continuous air raids in an attempt to gain control of British skies and prepare for a possible invasion. But on this day, British radar and fighter squadrons anticipated and countered the German offensive.

By the end of the battle, over 60 German aircraft had been shot down. British losses were far fewer. The RAF's strong defence convinced Hitler to postpone and eventually cancel his plans to invade Britain.

The victory was a major morale boost for Britain and demonstrated that the Nazis could be stopped. Winston Churchill praised the RAF with the famous words, "Never in the field of human conflict was so much owed by so many to so few."

September 16

Wall Street bombing kills dozens - 1920

On September 16, 1920, a horse-drawn wagon packed with explosives detonated on Wall Street in New York City's financial district, killing 38 people and injuring hundreds more. It was the deadliest terror attack in the United States at the time.

The explosion occurred during the lunch rush, just outside the offices of major banks and the New York Stock Exchange. The force of the blast shattered windows, flung debris across the street, and caused chaos in the heart of American capitalism.

Investigators blamed anarchists who were angry about the imprisonment of political radicals, but no one was ever convicted. The bombing shocked the country and heightened fears of domestic terrorism and political extremism.

Though Wall Street quickly reopened for business, the scars from the explosion lingered. The building of J.P. Morgan & Co. still bears pockmarks from the blast today.

September 17

King Charles VI orders expulsion of Jews from France - 1394

On September 17, 1394, King Charles VI of France issued a royal decree expelling all Jews from his kingdom. This act was the final in a series of medieval expulsions and marked the end of centuries of Jewish life in France — at least for a time.

Accusations against Jewish communities ranged from economic resentment to religious prejudice, often inflamed by church leaders. Although Jews had already faced restrictions on property ownership and moneylending, the crown now ordered them to leave entirely. They were given short notice to sell their possessions and depart.

This expulsion followed earlier removals under kings Philip II and Philip IV, but Charles VI's order was intended to be permanent. It drove thousands of Jewish families into exile, many seeking refuge in Italy, Spain, and Eastern Europe.

France would not officially allow Jews to return and resettle until the late 18th century under the reforms of the French Revolution. The 1394 expulsion reflects the deep intolerance and instability that Jewish communities faced across medieval Europe.

September 18

Great Fire of Moscow burns out after five days - 1812

On September 18, 1812, the devastating Great Fire of Moscow finally burned out after raging for five days and destroying nearly three-quarters of the Russian capital. The fire followed the city's occupation by Napoleon Bonaparte's Grand Army during his invasion of Russia.

As the French entered Moscow on September 14, they expected to find shelter and supplies. Instead, they found a mostly deserted city. Soon after, fires mysteriously broke out across the city. Many historians believe Russian military leaders or residents set the fires deliberately to deprive the French of resources.

The blaze engulfed homes, markets, and landmarks. Around 12,000 people were killed, and thousands more were left homeless. Napoleon, trapped in a burning city with no supplies, realized he could not stay.

The fire marked a turning point in the campaign. Unable to survive the Russian winter without support, Napoleon was forced to begin his disastrous retreat. The destruction of Moscow became one of the defining moments in the fall of the French Empire.

September 19

Lord William Bentinck outlaws Sati in India - 1829

On September 19, 1829, Governor-General Lord William Bentinck formally outlawed the practice of Sati — the ritual in which widows were expected to burn themselves alive on their husband's funeral pyre and in territories under British control in India.

Sati had existed for centuries and was especially common among certain Hindu communities. While not required by Hindu scripture, it was often enforced by local customs and social pressure. Reformers like Raja Ram Mohan Roy had spoken out strongly against the practice, calling it cruel and inhumane.

Bentinck's law criminalized anyone involved in encouraging or forcing a woman to commit Sati. The move angered some conservative groups but was widely praised by reformers.

Though the practice didn't disappear overnight, the ban marked a major step forward for women's rights in colonial India and remains one of the most significant reforms of British rule in the region.

September 20

Billie Jean King defeats Bobby Riggs in "Battle of the Sexes" - 1973

On September 20, 1973, tennis champion Billie Jean King beat Bobby Riggs in a widely publicized match known as the "Battle of the Sexes." Played in Houston, Texas, the event was more than a game and it became a symbol of the women's liberation movement.

Riggs, a former Wimbledon champion, had claimed that women's tennis was inferior and that even at age 55 he could beat any top female player. King, 29 at the time, accepted the challenge to prove him wrong.

In front of over 30,000 spectators and 90 million television viewers, King won in straight sets. Her victory was a powerful statement about gender equality in sports and beyond.

The match helped legitimize women's professional tennis and encouraged more support for female athletes. Billie Jean King became an icon not just for her skill, but for her role in pushing for equal treatment on and off the court.

September 21

Belize gains independence from the United Kingdom - 1981

On September 21, 1981, the Central American country of Belize officially gained independence from British colonial rule. Formerly known as British Honduras, Belize had been under British control since the 19th century.

As decolonization swept the globe in the post–World War II era, Belize gradually moved toward self-governance. A new constitution was adopted, and George Price became the first Prime Minister of an independent Belize.

Although independence was peaceful, it came with challenges. Guatemala had long claimed sovereignty over Belizean territory, leading to ongoing tensions. Britain retained a military presence for years to help defend the new nation.

Today, Belize is a member of the Commonwealth and maintains strong diplomatic and economic ties with both the Caribbean and Central America. Its independence day remains a major national holiday and a symbol of self-determination.

September 22

President Lincoln issues preliminary Emancipation Proclamation - 1862

On September 22, 1862, during the American Civil War, President Abraham Lincoln issued the preliminary Emancipation Proclamation. It declared that enslaved people in the rebelling Southern states would be set free if those states did not rejoin the Union by January 1, 1863.

The proclamation shifted the purpose of the war. What had started as a battle to preserve the Union now included the abolition of slavery. Though it didn't immediately free all enslaved people, it paved the way for freedom and allowed African Americans to join the Union Army.

The announcement received mixed reactions. Abolitionists cheered, while many in the South were furious. Some in the North feared it would prolong the war. But Lincoln stood firm, calling it a necessary war measure and a moral duty.

The final Emancipation Proclamation came into effect on New Year's Day, 1863, and was a crucial step toward the eventual end of slavery in the United States.

September 23

Nintendo is founded in Japan - 1889

On September 23, 1889, Fusajiro Yamauchi founded a small company in Kyoto, Japan, to produce handmade playing cards called *hanafuda*. The company was called Nintendo Koppai and it would one day become one of the biggest names in video gaming.

For decades, Nintendo sold cards and toys. It wasn't until the 1970s that it entered the electronic entertainment world. The company saw enormous success with arcade games like *Donkey Kong* and home consoles like the Famicom (NES).

In the 1980s and 1990s, Nintendo became a household name worldwide with franchises like *Super Mario*, *The Legend of Zelda*, and *Pokémon*. Its consoles revolutionized gaming culture and inspired generations.

From humble card-making beginnings to global entertainment powerhouse, Nintendo's journey spans over a century. The company's legacy continues to evolve, but it all began in 1889 with a simple deck of cards.

September 24

Black Friday gold panic hits U.S. markets - 1869

On September 24, 1869, known as Black Friday, the U.S. gold market collapsed after a failed attempt by financiers Jay Gould and James Fisk to corner the market. Their scheme caused financial panic and exposed corruption at the highest levels of business and politics.

Gould and Fisk had been buying massive amounts of gold, hoping to drive up the price and sell at a huge profit. They believed President Ulysses S. Grant would not interfere. But when the government realized what was happening, Grant ordered the Treasury to sell gold reserves.

The sudden flood of government gold caused prices to plummet. Investors who had bought in at high prices lost fortunes. The scandal rocked Wall Street and damaged public confidence in the economy.

Although Gould and Fisk escaped serious punishment, the crash led to calls for stronger regulation and transparency. Black Friday remains a warning of what can happen when unchecked greed meets weak oversight.

September 25

Central High School integrated in Little Rock, Arkansas - 1957

On September 25, 1957, nine African American students, known as the Little Rock Nine, entered Central High School in Little Rock, Arkansas, under the protection of U.S. Army troops. It was a landmark moment in the struggle for civil rights in America.

Earlier that month, the students had been blocked from entering the school by the Arkansas National Guard on the orders of Governor Orval Faubus, who opposed integration. In response, President Dwight D. Eisenhower sent federal troops to enforce the Supreme Court's ruling in *Brown v. Board of Education*, which had declared segregation in public schools unconstitutional.

Despite facing threats, harassment, and constant hostility, the nine teenagers courageously attended classes and paved the way for desegregation across the country.

The events in Little Rock showed that enforcing civil rights would require federal intervention, and they marked a turning point in the American civil rights movement.

September 26

First televised presidential debate held in the United States - 1960

On September 26, 1960, over 70 million Americans watched the first-ever televised U.S. presidential debate between Senator John F. Kennedy and Vice President Richard Nixon. It was a groundbreaking moment that changed the way political campaigns were run.

The debate highlighted the power of television. Kennedy appeared calm, confident, and charismatic, while Nixon, who was recovering from illness, looked pale and uneasy. Although many who listened on the radio thought Nixon had won, television viewers favoured Kennedy.

The debate gave Kennedy a major boost in a very close election and set the standard for all future presidential debates.

It also demonstrated how media could shape public perception, turning image and presentation into key parts of political success. From that point on, candidates needed to master not just policies, but performance.

September 27

Google officially founded - 1998

On September 27, 1998, two Stanford University students, Larry Page and Sergey Brin, officially founded Google, a search engine that would go on to revolutionize the internet and the world.

The pair had started the project as a research idea in 1996, aiming to improve web search by ranking pages based on how often other sites linked to them. The result was a faster, more relevant search engine that quickly became popular.

Operating out of a garage in California, Google began to grow rapidly. Its clean design and powerful algorithm made it stand out. Before long, it expanded into email, maps, advertising, smartphones, and artificial intelligence.

Today, Google is one of the most influential technology companies in history, with billions of users across the globe. What began as a college project on this day became a cornerstone of modern life.

September 28

William the Conqueror invades England - 1066

On September 28, 1066, William, Duke of Normandy, landed with thousands of troops on the southern coast of England. His goal was to claim the English throne, sparking one of the most important invasions in British history.

William believed he had a rightful claim to the crown after the death of King Edward the Confessor. But Harold Godwinson had been crowned king instead. Determined to take the throne, William launched a full-scale invasion.

His army landed near Pevensey and began preparing for battle. Less than three weeks later, they would face Harold's forces at the Battle of Hastings on October 14.

William's successful conquest reshaped English society, law, and language. Norman rule introduced a new aristocracy, built castles across the land, and laid the foundations of modern England.

September 29

First regular television broadcast in the U.K. - 1929

On September 29, 1929, the British Broadcasting Corporation (BBC) made its first experimental television transmission, marking the start of regular TV broadcasting in the United Kingdom.

The broadcast used mechanical television technology, which was still in its infancy. The images were crude and small, with very low resolution. However, it was a major technological breakthrough and a sign of things to come.

John Logie Baird, a Scottish engineer and television pioneer, had already demonstrated moving images years earlier. Now, with the BBC's involvement, television began transitioning from a science experiment to a public service.

Within a decade, television would begin to enter British homes. By the 1950s, it would become a central part of life, entertainment, and news across the country.

September 30

James Dean dies in car crash - 1955

On September 30, 1955, actor James Dean died in a car accident in California at the age of 24. His sudden death shocked the world and cemented his status as a cultural icon.

Dean had quickly risen to fame with starring roles in *Rebel Without a Cause*, *East of Eden*, and *Giant*. He became the symbol of youthful rebellion, capturing the spirit of a restless postwar generation.

On the day of his death, Dean was driving his Porsche 550 Spyder to a car race when he collided with another vehicle at high speed. He was killed almost instantly.

Although his film career lasted only a few years, Dean's impact on cinema and pop culture was immense. He became a legend and remains iconic to this day.

October 1

People's Republic of China founded - 1949

On October 1, 1949, Chairman Mao Zedong stood in Tiananmen Square and declared the founding of the People's Republic of China. It marked the end of a brutal civil war and the start of communist rule in the world's most populous nation.

The Chinese Communist Party had spent years fighting both the Japanese invaders and the Nationalist government, led by Chiang Kai-shek. After the Nationalists retreated to Taiwan, the Communists took control of mainland China.

Mao's announcement signalled a radical transformation. Land was redistributed, industries nationalized, and traditional institutions dismantled. Over the following decades, China experienced both major upheaval and enormous change.

October 1 remains China's National Day, celebrated with military parades and patriotic displays. It marks a defining moment in 20th-century history.

October 2

Mohandas Gandhi born in India - 1869

On October 2, 1869, Mohandas Karamchand Gandhi was born in Porbandar, India. Known to millions as Mahatma Gandhi, he became the leader of India's nonviolent movement for independence from British rule.

Educated in law in London and South Africa, Gandhi developed a philosophy of *satyagraha*, or nonviolent resistance. He led mass campaigns, including the Salt March and Quit India Movement, urging Indians to resist British control through peaceful protest.

His efforts inspired civil rights leaders around the world, including Martin Luther King Jr. and Nelson Mandela. Gandhi's methods proved that great political change could be achieved without violence.

He was assassinated in 1948, shortly after India gained independence. Today, Gandhi's birthday is a national holiday in India and is also observed as the International Day of Non-Violence.

October 3

Germany reunified after Cold War - 1990

On October 3, 1990, East and West Germany were officially reunified, ending four decades of division that had begun after World War II. The date is now celebrated as German Unity Day.

Germany had been split into two states during the Cold War which was West Germany, aligned with the West, and East Germany, under Soviet influence. The Berlin Wall had symbolized that division since 1961.

Following the fall of the wall in 1989 and the collapse of communist governments across Eastern Europe, momentum grew for reunification. After months of negotiations, the two German states joined together as one democratic nation.

Reunification was both hopeful and challenging. Economically and socially, it took years to rebuild a unified Germany. But politically, it marked the true end of the Cold War and the restoration of national identity.

October 4

Sputnik 1 becomes first satellite in space - 1957

On October 4, 1957, the Soviet Union launched *Sputnik 1*, the first artificial satellite to orbit the Earth. It marked the start of the space age and the space race between the United States and the USSR.

Sputnik 1 was a small, metal sphere with four antennas. It transmitted a steady radio signal that could be picked up around the globe. Although it only operated for 21 days, its impact was massive.

The launch stunned the world and caused panic in the United States, which feared it was falling behind in science and technology. In response, the U.S. created NASA and invested heavily in education and research.

The success of *Sputnik* showed the power of space exploration and triggered decades of competition and discovery. It was the first step toward space stations, moon landings, and interplanetary missions.

October 5

Wright brothers' first public flight in Europe - 1908

On October 5, 1908, Wilbur Wright amazed a crowd in Le Mans, France, with the first public demonstration of a Wright brothers airplane in Europe. Until then, many Europeans doubted that the Wrights had truly flown at all.

Wilbur's flight lasted over 9 minutes and covered several circuits around a field, proving beyond doubt that powered flight was real and controlled flight was possible. This demonstration changed aviation history.

The Wrights had achieved their first successful flight in 1903 in North Carolina, but their early work had not received much recognition outside the United States. Wilbur's 1908 flight captured headlines and silenced critics.

This event marked the beginning of international interest in aviation. It also led to contracts for building airplanes and inspired a generation of inventors and aviators around the world.

October 6

Yom Kippur War begins in the Middle East - 1973

On October 6, 1973, Egyptian and Syrian forces launched a surprise attack on Israel, starting what became known as the Yom Kippur War. The conflict began on Yom Kippur, the holiest day in Judaism, catching Israeli forces off guard.

The war was a response to Israel's victory in the Six-Day War of 1967, during which it had captured the Sinai Peninsula and the Golan Heights. In 1973, Egypt and Syria aimed to reclaim that lost territory.

For several days, the fighting was intense and bloody on both sides. Eventually, Israeli forces pushed back and gained ground. However, the war shook Israeli confidence and led to political changes in the region.

The conflict also drew in the United States and the Soviet Union, raising Cold War tensions. Although the war ended in a ceasefire, it set the stage for future peace talks and shifted the balance in Middle Eastern politics.

October 7

Vladimir Putin becomes acting president of Russia for the first time - 1999

On October 7, 1999, Vladimir Putin turned 47 years old. That same year, he had been appointed prime minister by President Boris Yeltsin and was already widely expected to become Russia's next leader.

Though he would not officially become acting president until December, October 1999 was when his rise to power truly began. At that time, he was virtually unknown to the public, but he gained popularity through strong rhetoric and a tough stance in the Second Chechen War.

By the end of the year, Yeltsin would step down unexpectedly, making Putin acting president. He then won the presidential election in March 2000.

From that point onward, Putin would dominate Russian politics for decades, with his leadership shaping Russia's internal policies and international relations into the 21st century.

October 8

Great Chicago Fire begins - 1871

On the night of October 8, 1871, a devastating fire broke out in Chicago, Illinois. What started as a small blaze quickly turned into one of the most destructive fires in American history.

The fire raged for more than 24 hours, fuelled by strong winds, dry weather, and wooden buildings. It destroyed over 17,000 structures, left 100,000 people homeless, and killed around 300.

Legend says it began in a barn owned by the O'Leary family, possibly kicked off by a cow, but the exact cause was never confirmed. What is certain is that Chicago was left in ruins.

Despite the destruction, the city rebuilt rapidly and came back stronger. In the years that followed, Chicago became a symbol of American resilience and innovation, with a skyline that would later be filled with some of the world's first skyscrapers.

October 9

Che Guevara executed in Bolivia - 1967

On October 9, 1967, revolutionary leader Ernesto "Che" Guevara was executed in Bolivia. Captured the day before by Bolivian forces with the help of the CIA, Guevara's death marked the end of his campaign to spread revolution in South America.

Born in Argentina, Guevara had gained fame as one of Fidel Castro's top commanders during the Cuban Revolution. After helping establish communist rule in Cuba, he left to support revolutions abroad.

In Bolivia, he tried to lead a guerrilla movement against the government. However, his efforts failed, and his group was hunted down in the jungle.

Che's death turned him into a global symbol of rebellion. His image which was wearing a beret and staring boldly ahead became iconic, appearing on posters, t-shirts, and murals around the world. His legacy remains controversial but undeniably powerful.

October 10

Taiwan celebrates Double Ten Day - 1911

October 10 is celebrated as Double Ten Day in Taiwan, marking the start of the Wuchang Uprising in 1911. This uprising sparked the revolution that overthrew China's last imperial dynasty, the Qing.

The rebellion began in the city of Wuchang when revolutionary forces, inspired by Sun Yat-sen's ideas, rose up against the Qing rulers. It quickly spread across China and led to the abdication of the last emperor, Puyi, just a few months later.

In 1912, the Republic of China was officially established, with Sun Yat-sen as its first provisional president. This was a turning point in Chinese history, ending over two thousand years of imperial rule.

Although the government of the Republic of China eventually relocated to Taiwan after the Chinese Civil War, Double Ten Day remains the country's national holiday and a powerful reminder of its revolutionary origins.

October 11

Apollo 7 launched into space - 1968

On October 11, 1968, NASA launched Apollo 7, the first successful crewed mission in the Apollo program. It was a crucial step in America's goal of landing astronauts on the Moon.

Apollo 7 carried astronauts Wally Schirra, Donn Eisele, and Walter Cunningham. Their mission was to test the redesigned spacecraft following the tragic Apollo 1 fire that had killed three astronauts the year before.

The flight lasted 11 days and orbited the Earth 163 times. The crew conducted important tests and even made the first live TV broadcasts from a U.S. spacecraft.

Apollo 7 proved that NASA's redesigned capsule was ready. It paved the way for future missions, including the famous Apollo 11 Moon landing less than a year later. The mission helped restore public confidence in the space program after earlier setbacks.

October 12

Columbus reaches the Americas - 1492

On October 12, 1492, Christopher Columbus made landfall on an island in the Bahamas, believing he had found a new route to Asia. Instead, he had reached the Americas, setting off a wave of exploration and colonization.

Columbus had sailed west from Spain with three ships: the Niña, the Pinta, and the Santa María. After more than a month at sea, the crew finally spotted land.

Although indigenous peoples had lived in the Americas for thousands of years, Columbus's voyage marked the beginning of lasting contact between Europe and the Western Hemisphere.

His arrival had massive consequences. While it opened the Americas to European trade and settlement, it also led to colonization, disease, and the destruction of native civilizations. Columbus remains a controversial figure, celebrated by some and criticized by others.

October 13

Hundreds of Knights Templar arrested in France - 1307

On October 13, 1307, hundreds of members of the Knights Templar were arrested in France by order of King Philip IV. The sudden crackdown shocked Europe and began the downfall of the powerful religious military order.

The Templars had been founded during the Crusades to protect pilgrims traveling to the Holy Land. Over time, they gained wealth and influence, operating like a medieval bank and owning land across Europe.

King Philip, deep in debt to the Templars, accused them of heresy, idol worship, and other crimes. Many were tortured into confessions, and dozens were eventually executed.

The arrests happened on a Friday, giving rise to the superstition around Friday the 13th being unlucky. The order was officially dissolved in 1312, but legends and conspiracy theories about the Templars have continued for centuries.

October 14

Battle of Hastings changes English history - 1066

On October 14, 1066, William, Duke of Normandy, defeated King Harold II of England at the Battle of Hastings. This victory gave William the English crown and changed the country forever.

The battle took place after King Edward the Confessor died without an heir. Harold claimed the throne, but William argued he had been promised it. William invaded England with a Norman army and met Harold's forces near Hastings.

The battle was fierce and bloody. According to tradition, Harold was killed by an arrow to the eye. With his death, English resistance collapsed.

William was crowned king on Christmas Day 1066. His victory introduced Norman rule, brought French influence to the English language, and reshaped the country's laws and society. The effects of the conquest can still be seen today.

October 15

First successful printing press introduced - 1452

Around October 15, 1452, German inventor Johannes Gutenberg began using his printing press to produce the Gutenberg Bible. It was the first major book printed with movable type in Europe.

Before this invention, books were copied by hand, which took months or even years. Gutenberg's press changed that by allowing texts to be reproduced quickly and accurately.

The Gutenberg Bible was beautifully made, and about 180 copies were produced. Its success proved the power of the printing press.

This invention sparked a communications revolution. It led to the spread of literacy, the Reformation, the scientific revolution, and eventually the rise of modern newspapers and books. Gutenberg's work is considered one of the greatest inventions in history.

October 16

Marie Antoinette executed during French Revolution - 1793

On October 16, 1793, Queen Marie Antoinette of France was executed by guillotine in Paris. Once a symbol of royal luxury, she became one of the most famous victims of the French Revolution.

Born in Austria, she married Louis XVI and became Queen of France. As revolution spread, the royal family was imprisoned and eventually put on trial. Louis was executed in January, and Marie Antoinette followed nine months later.

She was found guilty of high treason. Her trial was harsh and public, and she was taken to the guillotine in a simple cart, wearing a plain dress.

Her death marked the violent shift from monarchy to republic. Though she was hated by many at the time, later generations saw her as a tragic figure caught in the chaos of a revolution.

October 17

Loma Prieta earthquake hits California - 1989

On October 17, 1989, a powerful earthquake struck Northern California just before the start of a World Series baseball game in San Francisco. Known as the Loma Prieta earthquake, it caused widespread damage and killed 63 people.

The quake had a magnitude of 6.9 and lasted for about 15 seconds. It caused freeway collapses, fires, and severe destruction in the Bay Area. The city of Santa Cruz was hit especially hard.

Because many people were watching the World Series between the Giants and the A's, media coverage was extensive. The live television broadcast showed the screen shaking and then cutting out.

Despite the devastation, emergency response was quick, and the event led to improved building codes and disaster planning in the region.

October 18

Alaska formally transferred from Russia to the U.S. - 1867

On October 18, 1867, the United States formally took possession of Alaska from Russia. The transfer ceremony took place in Sitka, where the Russian flag was lowered and the American flag raised.

The U.S. had purchased Alaska for $7.2 million, a deal negotiated by Secretary of State William Seward. At the time, many people mocked the purchase, calling it "Seward's Folly," since Alaska seemed like a frozen wasteland.

However, the discovery of gold and later oil proved the value of the territory. Alaska eventually became the 49th state in 1959.

Today, October 18 is celebrated as Alaska Day. It marks the moment when the vast and resource-rich land officially became part of the United States.

October 19

British surrender at Yorktown ends major fighting in American Revolution - 1781

On October 19, 1781, British General Lord Cornwallis surrendered to American and French forces at Yorktown, Virginia. This decisive event effectively ended major combat in the American Revolutionary War.

The siege at Yorktown had lasted for weeks, with American troops under George Washington and French forces led by General Rochambeau surrounding the British. With no hope of reinforcement and supplies dwindling, Cornwallis had no choice but to capitulate.

Although the Treaty of Paris wouldn't be signed until 1783, the surrender at Yorktown marked the last significant battle of the war. The victory boosted American morale and solidified international support for the fledgling United States.

This moment is often remembered as the birth of American independence, with the surrender ceremony symbolizing the end of British colonial rule in the thirteen colonies.

October 20

Sydney Opera House officially opens - 1973

On October 20, 1973, the Sydney Opera House was officially opened by Queen Elizabeth II. The iconic structure, with its distinctive sail-like design, quickly became a symbol of Australia.

Designed by Danish architect Jørn Utzon, the project faced numerous challenges, including budget overruns and construction delays. Despite these issues, the finished building was celebrated for its innovative architecture and stunning location on Sydney Harbour.

The opening ceremony featured a grand performance and was attended by dignitaries from around the world. Since then, the Opera House has hosted countless performances and remains a centrepiece of Australia's cultural life.

Its unique design and cultural significance have earned it a place on the UNESCO World Heritage List, making it one of the most recognized and photographed buildings globally.

October 21

Battle of Trafalgar secures British naval supremacy - 1805

On October 21, 1805, the British Royal Navy, under Admiral Lord Nelson, achieved a decisive victory over the combined French and Spanish fleets at the Battle of Trafalgar.

Fought off the coast of Spain, the battle thwarted Napoleon Bonaparte's plans to invade Britain. Nelson's innovative tactics led to the destruction of much of the enemy fleet, ensuring British control of the seas.

Tragically, Admiral Nelson was mortally wounded during the battle. His leadership and sacrifice became legendary, and he was honoured as a national hero.

The victory at Trafalgar established British naval dominance for over a century, allowing the British Empire to expand its influence across the globe.

October 22

Cuban Missile Crisis begins with U.S. naval blockade - 1962

On October 22, 1962, President John F. Kennedy announced a naval blockade of Cuba in response to the discovery of Soviet nuclear missiles on the island. This marked the beginning of the Cuban Missile Crisis.

The world stood on the brink of nuclear war as the United States and the Soviet Union faced off. For thirteen tense days, negotiations continued behind the scenes while military forces were on high alert.

Eventually, the crisis was defused when the Soviet Union agreed to remove the missiles in exchange for a U.S. pledge not to invade Cuba and the secret removal of American missiles from Turkey.

The Cuban Missile Crisis is often cited as the closest the world has come to nuclear conflict, highlighting the importance of diplomacy and communication during times of international tension.

October 23

Beirut barracks bombing kills 241 U.S. service members - 1983

On October 23, 1983, a suicide truck bomber attacked the U.S. Marine barracks in Beirut, Lebanon, killing 241 American service members. Almost simultaneously, another bomber struck a French military compound, killing 58 paratroopers.

The attacks were carried out by Islamist militants opposed to the multinational peacekeeping force stationed in Lebanon during its civil war. The bombings marked one of the deadliest days for the U.S. military since World War II.

In response, the United States withdrew its forces from Lebanon, leading to debates about U.S. involvement in foreign conflicts and the risks faced by peacekeeping troops.

The tragedy underscored the vulnerabilities of military personnel in volatile regions and had lasting impacts on U.S. foreign policy in the Middle East.

October 24

United Nations officially established - 1945

On October 24, 1945, the United Nations was officially established following the ratification of its charter by the majority of its signatories, including the five permanent members of the Security Council.

Formed in the aftermath of World War II, the UN aimed to prevent future global conflicts and promote international cooperation. Its creation marked a significant step toward a more organized approach to global governance.

Since its inception, the UN has played a central role in peacekeeping, humanitarian aid, and the promotion of human rights. October 24 is celebrated annually as United Nations Day.

The organization's headquarters in New York City serves as a hub for diplomatic activity, bringing together representatives from nearly every nation to address global challenges.

October 25

Battle of Agincourt sees English victory over French - 1415

On October 25, 1415, during the Hundred Years' War, English forces led by King Henry V achieved a significant victory over the French at the Battle of Agincourt.

Despite being outnumbered and facing difficult conditions, the English army utilized longbowmen to devastating effect. The muddy battlefield hindered the heavily armoured French knights, leading to a catastrophic defeat.

The victory boosted English morale and solidified Henry V's reputation as a formidable military leader. The battle has been immortalized in literature, notably in Shakespeare's play "Henry V."

Agincourt remains one of the most celebrated military triumphs in English history, symbolizing the effectiveness of strategy and discipline over sheer numbers.

October 26

Hungarian Revolution begins with mass protests - 1956

On October 26, 1956, mass protests erupted in Hungary as citizens demanded political reform and an end to Soviet domination. The uprising quickly escalated into a nationwide revolt.

Demonstrators called for free elections, freedom of speech, and the withdrawal of Soviet troops. Initially, the government appeared to concede to some demands, but the situation remained volatile.

By early November, Soviet forces launched a massive military intervention to suppress the revolution. Thousands were killed, and many more fled the country as refugees.

The Hungarian Revolution highlighted the deep dissatisfaction with Soviet control in Eastern Europe and inspired future movements for freedom and independence.

October 27

New York City subway opens to the public - 1904

On October 27, 1904, New York City's first underground subway line opened to the public, marking a significant advancement in urban transportation.

The initial route ran from City Hall to 145th Street, covering nine miles and featuring 28 stations. Operated by the Interborough Rapid Transit Company (IRT), the subway quickly became a vital part of the city's infrastructure.

The success of the subway led to rapid expansion, transforming how New Yorkers commuted and shaping the city's growth. Today, the NYC subway system is one of the largest and busiest in the world.

Its introduction revolutionized urban transit and set a precedent for other cities worldwide.

October 28

Statue of Liberty dedicated in New York Harbor - 1886

On October 28, 1886, the Statue of Liberty was officially dedicated in New York Harbor. A gift from France, the statue symbolized freedom and democracy.

Designed by French sculptor Frédéric Auguste Bartholdi and built by Gustave Eiffel, the statue stands on Liberty Island and quickly became an iconic representation of the United States.

The dedication ceremony, attended by thousands, included speeches, a military parade, and the unveiling of the statue. Over time, it became a welcoming sight for immigrants arriving by sea.

The Statue of Liberty remains a powerful symbol of hope and liberty, recognized around the world.

October 29

Stock market crash triggers Great Depression - 1929

On October 29, 1929, known as "Black Tuesday," the U.S. stock market experienced a catastrophic crash, signalling the start of the Great Depression.

Panic selling led to a massive drop in stock prices, wiping out billions of dollars in wealth. The economic collapse had far-reaching effects, leading to widespread unemployment and hardship.

The Great Depression lasted for a decade, reshaping economies and societies worldwide. It prompted significant changes in financial regulations and government policies.

The events of Black Tuesday serve as a cautionary tale about the dangers of speculative bubbles and the importance of financial oversight.

October 30

Orson Welles' "War of the Worlds" radio broadcast causes panic - 1938

On October 30, 1938, Orson Welles broadcasted a radio adaptation of H.G. Wells' "The War of the Worlds," presenting it as a series of news bulletins. The realistic format led many listeners to believe that an actual Martian invasion was occurring.

The broadcast caused widespread panic, with some people fleeing their homes and others flooding emergency services with calls. Although the extent of the hysteria has been debated, the incident highlighted the power of media.

Welles' production became a landmark in broadcasting history, demonstrating the influence of radio and the importance of media literacy.

The event remains a fascinating example of how storytelling can blur the lines between fiction and reality.

October 31

Mount Rushmore project completed - 1941

On October 31, 1941, the construction of Mount Rushmore in South Dakota was completed after 14 years of work. The monument features the carved faces of Presidents George Washington, Thomas Jefferson, Theodore Roosevelt, and Abraham Lincoln.

Sculptor Gutzon Borglum led the project, which aimed to promote tourism and commemorate American history. Despite challenges, including funding issues and Borglum's death before completion, the monument was finished under the direction of his son.

Mount Rushmore has become a symbol of American ideals and a popular tourist destination, attracting millions of visitors annually.

Its creation reflects both the ambition and complexity of national identity and memory.

November 1

Lisbon earthquake and tsunami devastate Portugal - 1755

On November 1, 1755, a massive earthquake struck Lisbon, Portugal, followed by a tsunami and fires that destroyed much of the city. It is considered one of the deadliest natural disasters in European history.

The quake struck in the morning during All Saints' Day Mass, toppling churches and buildings filled with worshippers. Moments later, a tsunami surged into the city, followed by days of fire. It is estimated that between 40,000 and 50,000 people died.

This disaster had far-reaching consequences. It deeply impacted European philosophy, sparking debate among Enlightenment thinkers about the role of divine intervention. It also led to major reforms in disaster response and urban planning under the leadership of the Marquis of Pombal.

The Lisbon earthquake reshaped not only the city itself but also European attitudes toward science, theology, and human resilience.

November 2

False report claims Mike Tyson is dead - 1988

On November 2, 1988, a Mexican radio station mistakenly reported that heavyweight boxing champion Mike Tyson had died in a car crash. The false news quickly spread across media outlets, causing widespread panic and confusion among fans.

At the time, Tyson was one of the most dominant and recognizable athletes in the world. He had recently defended his title and was seen as nearly unbeatable in the ring. The report claimed that he had been involved in a fatal accident in New York, which was entirely untrue.

Tyson was, in fact, alive and well. The hoax was quickly corrected, but not before major news organizations and sports fans had reacted with shock. The incident highlighted the dangers of broadcasting unverified news, especially in the age before instant internet corrections.

The event remains a bizarre moment in media history, showing how even global figures can be swept up in misinformation.

November 3

Sputnik 2 launches first living creature into orbit - 1957

On November 3, 1957, the Soviet Union launched Sputnik 2, carrying a living passenger into space for the first time: a dog named Laika.

Laika, a stray from the streets of Moscow, became the first animal to orbit Earth. Her mission was part of the early space race between the United States and the Soviet Union, coming just a month after the launch of Sputnik 1.

Although there was no plan to return Laika safely to Earth, her mission provided valuable information about the effects of spaceflight on living organisms. Sadly, Laika died a few hours into the flight from overheating.

Her story remains a poignant symbol of both scientific progress and ethical controversy. Today, monuments and memorials around the world commemorate her sacrifice.

November 4

Iranian militants seize U.S. Embassy in Tehran - 1979

On November 4, 1979, Iranian militants stormed the United States Embassy in Tehran, taking 66 American diplomats and citizens hostage. This marked the beginning of a 444-day crisis that would reshape U.S.-Iran relations.

The takeover followed Iran's Islamic Revolution and the U.S. decision to allow the exiled Shah to receive medical treatment in America. Many Iranians feared the U.S. would try to restore him to power, as it had in 1953.

The prolonged hostage crisis dominated news headlines and became a central issue in U.S. politics, contributing to President Jimmy Carter's electoral defeat in 1980. The hostages were finally released on January 20, 1981, the day Ronald Reagan took office.

The crisis left a lasting scar on diplomatic relations between the two nations and set the tone for decades of tension.

November 5

Gunpowder Plot to blow up British Parliament is foiled - 1605

On November 5, 1605, English authorities uncovered a plot to assassinate King James I by blowing up the House of Lords during the State Opening of Parliament. The discovery became known as the Gunpowder Plot.

Led by Robert Catesby and carried out by a group of English Catholics, the plot aimed to restore a Catholic monarch to the throne. Guy Fawkes, the most famous conspirator, was found guarding barrels of gunpowder beneath Parliament.

The plot failed, and the conspirators were either killed or executed. The event is still remembered in Britain each year as Guy Fawkes Night, with fireworks and bonfires.

The plot deepened religious divisions in England and led to stricter laws against Catholics, changing the course of British religious and political history.

November 6

Abraham Lincoln elected President of the United States - 1860

On November 6, 1860, Abraham Lincoln was elected as the 16th President of the United States. His victory set off a chain of events that would lead to the Civil War.

Lincoln, running as a Republican, opposed the expansion of slavery into new territories. His election alarmed Southern states, which saw it as a threat to their way of life. Within months, several states began seceding from the Union.

Though Lincoln did not initially call for the immediate abolition of slavery, his presidency became defined by the conflict that followed. His leadership preserved the Union and paved the way for the eventual emancipation of enslaved people.

His election remains a pivotal moment in American history, marking the start of the nation's most profound internal struggle.

November 7

Bolsheviks seize power during Russian Revolution - 1917

On November 7, 1917, Bolshevik forces led by Vladimir Lenin overthrew Russia's Provisional Government in what became known as the October Revolution (based on the Julian calendar then in use).

The Bolsheviks took control of key locations in Petrograd (now St. Petersburg), including government offices and the Winter Palace. The coup marked the beginning of communist rule in Russia and led to the creation of the Soviet Union.

The revolution followed months of unrest, food shortages, and dissatisfaction with Russia's role in World War I. The Bolsheviks promised peace, land reform, and workers' rights, gaining support from soldiers and industrial workers.

This dramatic shift altered global politics for the rest of the 20th century and led to decades of Cold War tensions.

November 8

Hitler attempts Beer Hall Putsch in Munich - 1923

On November 8, 1923, Adolf Hitler and members of the Nazi Party launched an attempted coup in Munich, known as the Beer Hall Putsch. The effort failed, but it marked a key moment in Hitler's rise to power.

Hitler and his followers tried to seize control of the Bavarian government by storming a beer hall where officials were gathered. The plan unraveled the next day when police confronted the rebels in the streets. Sixteen Nazis and four police officers were killed.

Hitler was arrested and sentenced to prison, where he wrote his political manifesto, *Mein Kampf*. Although the putsch failed, it gave Hitler national attention and allowed him to reframe himself as a political martyr.

Within a decade, he would legally rise to power and transform Germany through dictatorship.

November 9

Berlin Wall falls, ending decades of division - 1989

On November 9, 1989, the Berlin Wall, which had divided East and West Berlin since 1961, began to come down. The collapse marked the beginning of the end for Communist regimes across Eastern Europe.

Following weeks of protests and mounting pressure, East German authorities announced that citizens could freely cross into West Berlin. Crowds gathered at the wall, and guards opened the checkpoints. That night, people began dismantling the wall with hammers and picks.

The fall of the wall symbolized the collapse of Soviet influence and the triumph of democratic movements. Within a year, Germany was officially reunified.

It remains one of the most powerful moments in modern European history and a lasting symbol of freedom.

November 10

Martin Luther defies the Pope by burning the papal bull - 1520

On November 10, 1520, Martin Luther publicly burned the papal bull that condemned his writings and threatened him with excommunication. This act of defiance intensified the Reformation.

The document, issued by Pope Leo X, demanded that Luther recant his criticisms of the Catholic Church, especially those related to the sale of indulgences. Instead, Luther burned it in Wittenberg, declaring the pope's authority illegitimate.

Luther's bold move galvanized his followers and set the stage for a permanent split in Christianity. Within a few years, Protestant churches emerged across Europe.

His actions fundamentally altered the religious landscape of the continent and led to centuries of theological and political change.

November 11

World War I ends with armistice - 1918

On November 11, 1918, World War I came to an end with the signing of an armistice between the Allies and Germany. The agreement took effect at 11 a.m., bringing four years of brutal fighting to a close.

The war, which had claimed over 16 million lives, left Europe devastated. The armistice was signed in a railway carriage in the Forest of Compiègne, France. Celebrations erupted across the world as news of the ceasefire spread.

Though peace negotiations would continue into the next year, November 11 became a symbol of remembrance for the fallen. In many countries, it is observed as Armistice Day, Remembrance Day, or Veterans Day.

The legacy of the war shaped the 20th century and laid the groundwork for future global conflict.

November 12

Ellis Island closes as an immigration station - 1954

On November 12, 1954, Ellis Island officially closed its doors as an immigration processing station, ending a significant chapter in American history.

Located in New York Harbor, Ellis Island had served as the primary gateway for over 12 million immigrants entering the United States between 1892 and 1954. For many, it was the first experience of America, filled with hope, anxiety, and the promise of a new life.

After changes in immigration policy and improvements in transportation, the need for such a processing centre declined. The facility was eventually transformed into a museum and part of the Statue of Liberty National Monument.

Today, Ellis Island stands as a powerful symbol of America's immigrant roots and diverse cultural heritage.

November 13

First known use of "zero" in India is recorded - 628

On November 13, 628, a reference to the number zero appeared in a Sanskrit inscription in India. This is one of the earliest known uses of the concept as a numeral.

The inscription, found at the Chaturbhuj temple in Gwalior, uses zero in a mathematical context, showing advanced understanding of numbers and place value. Indian scholars had been developing the concept for centuries, and it eventually spread to the Islamic world and Europe.

The introduction of zero transformed mathematics, making complex calculations possible and forming the foundation of modern computing.

This small symbol represents one of humanity's most important intellectual breakthroughs.

November 14

Apollo 12 launches on second moon mission - 1969

On November 14, 1969, NASA launched Apollo 12, the second crewed mission to land on the Moon. Astronauts Charles "Pete" Conrad, Richard Gordon, and Alan Bean led the mission.

Launched just four months after Apollo 11, the mission aimed to demonstrate a more precise lunar landing. Despite being struck by lightning shortly after takeoff, the crew safely reached the Moon and conducted two moonwalks in the Ocean of Storms.

They collected lunar samples and deployed scientific instruments, helping scientists learn more about the Moon's composition and environment. The success of Apollo 12 proved the reliability of continued space exploration.

It reinforced the achievements of the Apollo program and contributed to America's legacy in space history.

November 15

Germany bombards London with V-2 rockets - 1944

On November 15, 1944, Nazi Germany launched a V-2 rocket attack on London, part of a terrifying new phase in World War II. The V-2 was the world's first long-range guided ballistic missile and represented a major leap in military technology.

The rocket struck London's southern suburbs, killing and injuring civilians without warning. Unlike earlier V-1 "buzz bombs," the V-2 traveled faster than the speed of sound, giving no audible sign of approach. Victims had no time to seek shelter.

Developed by Wernher von Braun and his team, the V-2 was launched from occupied territories and caused severe damage and panic. Although the weapon had limited impact on the war's outcome, it marked the dawn of modern missile warfare.

After the war, captured German scientists contributed to both American and Soviet rocket programs, laying the groundwork for the space race.

November 16

Oklahoma becomes the 46th U.S. state - 1907

On November 16, 1907, Oklahoma officially joined the United States as the 46th state. It was created from the combination of Oklahoma Territory and Indian Territory.

The land had been designated in the 19th century as a destination for Native American tribes who were forcibly relocated, most notably during the Trail of Tears. Over time, however, increasing numbers of settlers moved into the region, and the federal government opened parts of it to non-Native settlement.

Statehood followed years of legal negotiations, land runs, and political pressure. The new state adopted a constitution that blended frontier traditions with progressive reforms, including stronger labour laws and women's rights.

Oklahoma's path to statehood reflects a complex history of displacement, settlement, and change in the American West.

November 17

Velvet Revolution begins in Czechoslovakia - 1989

On November 17, 1989, peaceful student protests in Prague marked the start of the Velvet Revolution, a non-violent movement that led to the fall of Communist rule in Czechoslovakia.

The protest was organized to commemorate the anniversary of a 1939 student uprising against Nazi occupation. However, it quickly grew into a broader call for democratic reforms and human rights. Police cracked down, but the public response only grew stronger.

Over the following weeks, mass demonstrations spread across the country. By December, the Communist government resigned, and dissident leader Václav Havel became president.

The Velvet Revolution is remembered as one of the most successful peaceful transitions of power in modern European history.

November 18

Mass suicide at Jonestown shocks the world - 1978

On November 18, 1978, over 900 members of the Peoples Temple cult died in a mass murder-suicide in Jonestown, Guyana, orchestrated by their leader Jim Jones.

Jones, an American preacher, had moved his followers from California to a remote settlement in South America to escape scrutiny. When U.S. Congressman Leo Ryan visited to investigate, he and several others were shot and killed as they tried to leave.

In response, Jones ordered his followers to drink a cyanide-laced beverage. Most obeyed, including many children. The event remains one of the largest losses of American civilian life in a single incident outside of a natural disaster.

Jonestown became a chilling example of the dangers of cult leadership, manipulation, and blind obedience.

November 19

Lincoln delivers Gettysburg Address - 1863

On November 19, 1863, President Abraham Lincoln gave the Gettysburg Address during the dedication of a national cemetery at the site of one of the Civil War's bloodiest battles.

In just 272 words, Lincoln redefined the meaning of the war and the American experiment. He emphasized liberty, equality, and the idea that the Union's survival was essential to preserving democracy itself.

Though the speech was initially met with mixed reviews, it became one of the most famous and respected addresses in U.S. history. Its words continue to be taught, quoted, and remembered for their clarity and moral power.

The Gettysburg Address endures as a defining moment in the American story.

November 20

Nuremberg Trials begin for Nazi war crimes - 1945

On November 20, 1945, the first Nuremberg Trial began in Germany, where leading Nazi officials were prosecuted for crimes against humanity, war crimes, and genocide.

Held by the Allied powers, the trials represented a historic moment in international law. Twenty-four major Nazi leaders were put on trial before an international military tribunal. Prosecutors presented overwhelming evidence of atrocities, including the Holocaust.

The trials introduced the principle that individuals, not just states, could be held accountable for crimes during wartime. They also laid the foundation for later tribunals and the International Criminal Court.

The Nuremberg Trials marked a turning point in the pursuit of global justice.

November 21

Mayflower Compact signed by Pilgrims - 1620

On November 21, 1620 (by the Gregorian calendar), the Pilgrims aboard the *Mayflower* signed the Mayflower Compact, the first governing document of their new colony in North America.

Before disembarking at Plymouth, the settlers agreed to form a "civil body politic" and abide by laws made for the good of the colony. This compact was necessary because they had landed outside the territory covered by their original charter.

Although brief, the document established principles of self-government and majority rule. It served as an early model for democratic governance in America.

The Mayflower Compact is often seen as a founding step toward the development of the U.S. Constitution and the country's democratic ideals.

November 22

President John F. Kennedy assassinated - 1963

On November 22, 1963, President John F. Kennedy was assassinated while riding in a motorcade through Dallas, Texas. He was 46 years old.

Kennedy was struck by gunfire as his convertible passed through Dealey Plaza. Governor John Connally was also injured. Within hours, Vice President Lyndon B. Johnson was sworn in aboard Air Force One. Lee Harvey Oswald was arrested for the crime, but he was shot and killed two days later by nightclub owner Jack Ruby.

The assassination shocked the world and led to decades of investigation and conspiracy theories. For many, it marked the end of the postwar optimism of the early 1960s.

Kennedy's death became one of the most defining and tragic moments in American history.

November 23

First episode of Doctor Who airs on BBC - 1963

On November 23, 1963, the British Broadcasting Corporation aired the first episode of *Doctor Who*, launching what would become the longest-running science fiction television series in history.

The show introduced audiences to the mysterious Doctor, a time-traveling alien known as a Time Lord, who journeys through space and time in the TARDIS. The first episode, "An Unearthly Child," introduced the Doctor and his granddaughter Susan, along with two schoolteachers who become their companions.

Initially aimed at children, the show quickly became a cultural phenomenon. Its unique premise and ability to reinvent itself—thanks to the Doctor's power to regenerate—have allowed it to endure for decades.

Doctor Who remains a beloved part of global pop culture and British television history.

November 24

Charles Darwin publishes On the Origin of Species - 1859

On November 24, 1859, Charles Darwin published *On the Origin of Species*, introducing the theory of evolution by natural selection. The book revolutionized the biological sciences and changed how people viewed life on Earth.

Darwin had spent decades collecting evidence from his voyage aboard the HMS *Beagle*, where he observed species across South America and the Galápagos Islands. His central idea was that organisms evolve over time through a process of variation and survival of the fittest.

The book was both praised and controversial. It challenged religious views on creation and sparked intense debate in scientific and public circles.

Today, Darwin's work remains a cornerstone of modern biology and evolutionary science.

November 25

Christopher Columbus is arrested in Santo Domingo - 1500

On November 25, 1500, Christopher Columbus was arrested and taken into custody by Francisco de Bobadilla, the newly appointed governor of Santo Domingo on behalf of the Spanish Crown.

Columbus had been facing growing complaints about his brutal and ineffective governance of the colony. Spanish settlers accused him of tyranny, mismanagement, and cruelty, including violent treatment of both colonists and Indigenous peoples. King Ferdinand and Queen Isabella sent Bobadilla to investigate, and he wasted no time in seizing power and arresting Columbus and his brothers.

The explorer was sent back to Spain in chains. Although he was later released and granted another voyage, he never again held authority in the New World.

This event marked a sharp turning point in Columbus's legacy, revealing the darker aspects of his administration and the increasing control the Spanish Crown would exert over its overseas empire.

November 26

King Tut's tomb is opened by Howard Carter - 1922

On November 26, 1922, British archaeologist Howard Carter opened the sealed inner chamber of Tutankhamun's tomb in Egypt's Valley of the Kings. Inside, he found the nearly intact burial of the young pharaoh.

The tomb had been discovered weeks earlier, but this moment revealed the famous golden sarcophagus and treasures untouched for over 3,000 years. It was the most significant archaeological discovery of the 20th century.

Tutankhamun was a relatively minor king, but the wealth of artifacts in his tomb stunned the world and sparked a wave of fascination with ancient Egypt.

The find also ignited rumours of a "pharaoh's curse," which added mystery to an already legendary event.

November 27

Harvey Milk and George Moscone assassinated - 1978

On November 27, 1978, San Francisco Supervisor Harvey Milk and Mayor George Moscone were assassinated by former city supervisor Dan White at City Hall.

Milk was one of the first openly gay elected officials in the United States and a prominent advocate for LGBTQ rights. His assassination shocked the nation and led to protests and a greater push for equality.

Dan White was later convicted of voluntary manslaughter rather than murder, prompting outrage and the so-called White Night riots.

Milk's legacy continues through public service, activism, and a broader fight for civil rights across the country.

November 28

Mongols lay siege to Kyiv - 1240

On November 28, 1240, the Mongol army led by Batu Khan began its siege of Kyiv, the capital of Kievan Rus. After surrounding the city, the Mongols used catapults and siege engines to batter its fortifications.

The defenders, heavily outnumbered, resisted for several days. But the Mongols' advanced tactics and overwhelming force broke through. By December 6, the city fell. Thousands of civilians were massacred, and much of Kyiv was burned to the ground.

The sack of Kyiv marked the near-total collapse of Kievan Rus, once a powerful and influential medieval state. The Mongol invasion ushered in a period of foreign domination and fragmentation in the region.

The devastation of Kyiv was a turning point in Eastern European history, altering the course of Russian, Ukrainian, and Mongol political development.

November 29

Deadly uranium mine explosions in East Germany - 1949

On November 29, 1949, a series of deadly explosions occurred at uranium mines operated by the Soviet Union in the East German town of Johanngeorgenstadt. The blasts, poorly documented at the time, are believed to have killed over 3,700 miners.

These mines were part of the Wismut project, a top-secret Soviet-German operation supplying uranium for the USSR's nuclear weapons program. The work was dangerous, and safety standards were minimal. Explosions were caused by gas leaks and unstable blasting procedures in underground shafts.

Because of Cold War secrecy, details were covered up for decades. Survivors and families were denied recognition, and the full scale of the disaster was not acknowledged until long after German reunification.

The event remains one of the deadliest industrial accidents in European history and a grim reminder of Cold War-era exploitation and secrecy.

November 30

Winston Churchill is born in Blenheim Palace - 1874

On November 30, 1874, Winston Churchill was born at Blenheim Palace in Oxfordshire, England. He would go on to become one of the most important leaders of the 20th century.

Churchill held many political roles, but he is best remembered as Britain's Prime Minister during World War II. His speeches, determination, and leadership helped rally the British people during their darkest hours.

Beyond politics, Churchill was also a soldier, historian, and Nobel Prize-winning writer. He served as Prime Minister again in the early 1950s before retiring from public life.

His legacy is both complex and monumental, and his influence is still studied and debated around the world.

December 1

Rosa Parks refuses to give up her seat - 1955

On December 1, 1955, in Montgomery, Alabama, Rosa Parks was arrested for refusing to give up her seat to a white passenger on a segregated bus. Her quiet act of defiance became a powerful symbol of the civil rights movement.

Parks was not the first person to resist segregation, but her action came at a moment when local Black leaders were ready to organize. Within days, the Montgomery Bus Boycott was launched, led in part by a young pastor named Martin Luther King Jr.

The boycott lasted over a year and ended with the Supreme Court ruling that bus segregation was unconstitutional. Rosa Parks became a national icon, and her courage inspired many others to join the struggle for equality.

Her simple yet bold decision helped ignite one of the most important social movements in American history.

December 2

Napoleon crowns himself Emperor of France - 1804

On December 2, 1804, Napoleon Bonaparte crowned himself Emperor of the French in a lavish ceremony at Notre-Dame Cathedral in Paris. The event signalled the official transformation of the French Republic into an empire.

Pope Pius VII attended the coronation but played only a symbolic role. In a dramatic gesture, Napoleon took the crown from the pope's hands and placed it on his own head. This action declared that his power came not from the Church, but from himself and the people.

Napoleon's coronation ended a period of revolutionary turmoil and began an era of military conquest and centralized authority in France. His reign would reshape Europe and leave a complex legacy of reform, war, and nationalism.

December 3

First successful heart transplant is performed - 1967

On December 3, 1967, Dr. Christiaan Barnard and his team in Cape Town, South Africa, performed the world's first successful human heart transplant. The patient, Louis Washkansky, received the heart of a young woman who had died in a car accident.

Although Washkansky lived only 18 days due to pneumonia, the surgery proved that heart transplants were possible. It sparked a wave of medical innovation and opened new frontiers in organ transplantation.

Dr. Barnard became internationally famous, and his pioneering work laid the foundation for future improvements in surgical techniques and anti-rejection medications. Today, heart transplants save thousands of lives each year.

This breakthrough remains a milestone in medical history.

December 4

The Beatles release their final album in the UK - 1970

On December 4, 1970, *Let It Be*, the final studio album by The Beatles, was released in the United Kingdom. Although it had already come out in the United States in May, the UK release marked the end of the band's recording era.

The songs on the album were recorded before *Abbey Road* but were shelved due to internal tensions. Phil Spector later produced the final version, adding orchestration and new mixes that not all band members agreed with.

Despite the conflicts, *Let It Be* featured major hits like "The Long and Winding Road," "Get Back," and the title track. The album topped charts worldwide and became a bittersweet farewell for fans.

It was the closing chapter for the most influential band in modern music history.

December 5

Prohibition ends in the United States - 1933

On December 5, 1933, the 21st Amendment to the U.S. Constitution was ratified, officially repealing Prohibition. This ended 13 years of a nationwide ban on the sale, production, and transportation of alcohol.

Prohibition, enacted in 1920 through the 18th Amendment, aimed to reduce crime and improve health. Instead, it led to a rise in organized crime, bootlegging, and illegal speakeasies. Public support declined steadily during the 1920s.

The repeal was celebrated across the country, especially by breweries and distilleries eager to resume legal operations. It also gave the federal and state governments a new source of tax revenue during the Great Depression.

The end of Prohibition marked a major shift in American law and culture.

December 6

Explosion devastates Halifax, Canada - 1917

On December 6, 1917, the port city of Halifax, Nova Scotia, was rocked by the largest man-made explosion in history at that time. The blast occurred when a French cargo ship carrying explosives, the *Mont-Blanc*, collided with a Norwegian vessel in the harbour.

The resulting explosion levelled much of the city's north end, killed approximately 2,000 people, and injured thousands more. The shockwave shattered windows over ten miles away, and a tsunami caused additional destruction.

The Halifax Explosion was a devastating tragedy, but it also led to advances in emergency response and international aid. Help came from across Canada and even from the United States.

It remains one of the deadliest accidents in Canadian history.

December 7

Attack on Pearl Harbor brings U.S. into World War II - 1941

On December 7, 1941, Japanese aircraft launched a surprise military strike on the U.S. naval base at Pearl Harbor in Hawaii. The attack killed over 2,400 Americans and damaged or destroyed much of the Pacific Fleet.

The goal was to cripple U.S. naval power in the Pacific before Japan expanded further across Asia. However, the attack had the opposite effect. The very next day, the United States declared war on Japan, entering World War II.

President Franklin D. Roosevelt described it as "a date which will live in infamy." The attack united the American public and shifted the global balance of power.

Pearl Harbor remains one of the most significant events in U.S. military history.

December 8

John Lennon is murdered in New York City - 1980

On December 8, 1980, former Beatle John Lennon was shot and killed outside his apartment building, The Dakota, in New York City. He was 40 years old.

Lennon had recently returned to public life with a new album, *Double Fantasy*, and was walking home with his wife, Yoko Ono, when the shooter, Mark David Chapman, attacked him. Lennon was rushed to the hospital but pronounced dead on arrival.

The murder shocked fans around the world and sparked public mourning on a massive scale. Lennon was remembered not only as a musical legend but also as a peace activist and cultural icon.

His legacy endures through his music and message of peace.

December 9

World's first computer bug is recorded - 1947

On December 9, 1947, computer pioneer Grace Hopper and her team documented the first literal "computer bug." They found a moth trapped inside a relay of the Harvard Mark II computer, causing a malfunction.

They taped the moth into the logbook and wrote, "First actual case of bug being found." Although the term "bug" had been used informally in engineering before, this event helped popularize it in the context of computing.

Grace Hopper was a key figure in early programming and played a major role in developing the COBOL language. The story of the moth remains a quirky but important milestone in the history of technology.

December 10

Alfred Nobel dies, later inspires Nobel Prizes - 1896

On December 10, 1896, Alfred Nobel, the Swedish chemist and inventor of dynamite, died in San Remo, Italy. His death triggered the execution of his will, which created the Nobel Prizes.

Nobel had made a fortune from explosives but was troubled by their use in warfare. After a premature obituary called him the "merchant of death," he decided to leave most of his wealth to a fund recognizing achievements in peace, science, and literature.

The first Nobel Prizes were awarded in 1901. They have since become among the most prestigious honours in the world, promoting excellence and humanitarian progress.

Alfred Nobel's final legacy was one of peace, not destruction.

December 11

Edward VIII abdicates the British throne - 1936

On December 11, 1936, King Edward VIII became the first British monarch to voluntarily abdicate the throne. His decision was driven by his desire to marry Wallis Simpson, an American divorcée, which created a constitutional crisis.

As head of the Church of England, the king was not permitted to marry a divorced woman whose ex-husbands were still living. Facing pressure from the government and public, Edward chose love over duty.

He was succeeded by his brother, who became King George VI. Edward was given the title Duke of Windsor and spent most of his life in exile.

The abdication changed the course of royal history and eventually led to Queen Elizabeth II's long reign.

December 12

Kenya gains independence from Britain - 1963

On December 12, 1963, Kenya officially gained independence from British colonial rule. Jomo Kenyatta became the country's first Prime Minister and later its first President.

The road to independence was long and marked by resistance, most notably the Mau Mau uprising, which began in the 1950s. Thousands died during the struggle, and the British responded with brutal repression.

When independence finally came, celebrations were held across the country. The Kenyan flag was raised for the first time, replacing the Union Jack.

Kenya's independence was part of a broader wave of decolonization across Africa during the 20th century.

December 13

Al Gore concedes U.S. presidential election - 2000

On December 13, 2000, Vice President Al Gore conceded defeat to George W. Bush in the U.S. presidential election, ending one of the most contentious political battles in American history.

The election had come down to a razor-thin margin in Florida. After weeks of recounts and legal challenges, the Supreme Court ruled to stop further recounts, effectively awarding the state's electoral votes to Bush.

In a televised speech, Gore urged unity and accepted the decision "for the sake of our unity as a people and the strength of our democracy."

The election exposed flaws in the voting system and left a lasting impact on U.S. politics and election law.

December 14

South Pole is reached for the first time - 1911

On December 14, 1911, Norwegian explorer Roald Amundsen and his team became the first humans to reach the South Pole. They planted the Norwegian flag and left supplies for a planned return journey.

Amundsen's team beat a British expedition led by Robert Falcon Scott, who arrived nearly five weeks later and tragically died on the return trip. The success was due to careful planning, use of sled dogs, and Amundsen's experience in polar travel.

The achievement was a milestone in the age of exploration and brought global fame to Amundsen.

Reaching the South Pole remains one of the great triumphs of human endurance and navigation.

December 15

Bill of Rights is ratified in the United States - 1791

On December 15, 1791, the United States ratified the Bill of Rights, the first ten amendments to the Constitution. These amendments guaranteed essential liberties, including freedom of speech, religion, the press, and the right to a fair trial.

The Bill of Rights was created to address fears that the new federal government would have too much power. States had demanded these protections before agreeing to ratify the Constitution.

Drafted by James Madison, the amendments drew from Enlightenment ideas and earlier English legal traditions. They became the foundation of American civil rights law and are still central to legal debates and protections today.

Their ratification marked a defining moment in American democracy.

December 16

Boston Tea Party takes place - 1773

On December 16, 1773, American colonists disguised as Mohawk warriors boarded British ships in Boston Harbor and dumped 342 chests of tea into the water. This act of protest became known as the Boston Tea Party.

The colonists were protesting the Tea Act, which gave the British East India Company a monopoly on tea sales and imposed taxes without colonial representation. The dramatic act of defiance enraged British authorities and led to harsh penalties.

In response, Parliament passed the Coercive Acts, known in America as the Intolerable Acts, which pushed the colonies closer to open rebellion.

The Boston Tea Party became a powerful symbol of resistance and helped spark the American Revolutionary War.

December 17

Wright brothers make first powered flight - 1903

On December 17, 1903, Orville and Wilbur Wright made the first successful powered, controlled, and sustained flight in a heavier-than-air machine at Kitty Hawk, North Carolina.

Their aircraft, the Wright Flyer, stayed aloft for 12 seconds and travelled 120 feet. Later that day, they achieved longer flights, with the final one lasting 59 seconds and covering 852 feet.

The brothers' success was the result of years of experimentation and engineering, including innovations in wing design and control systems. Their breakthrough launched the age of aviation and eventually transformed transportation and warfare.

Today, their achievement is recognized as one of the most important milestones in human history.

December 18

Joseph Stalin is born in Georgia - 1878

On December 18, 1878, Joseph Stalin was born in Gori, Georgia, then part of the Russian Empire. He would become one of the most powerful and controversial leaders in world history.

Stalin rose through the ranks of the Communist Party after the Russian Revolution and became the de facto leader of the Soviet Union by the late 1920s. His rule was marked by rapid industrialization, brutal purges, forced collectivization, and mass famine.

During World War II, Stalin led the Soviet war effort against Nazi Germany. After the war, he oversaw the expansion of Soviet influence across Eastern Europe.

Stalin's policies caused the deaths of millions, and his legacy remains highly debated. He died in 1953, leaving behind a transformed but deeply scarred nation.

December 19

President Clinton is impeached - 1998

On December 19, 1998, the U.S. House of Representatives voted to impeach President Bill Clinton on charges of perjury and obstruction of justice. The case stemmed from his testimony about an affair with White House intern Monica Lewinsky.

Clinton was the second U.S. president to be impeached, after Andrew Johnson in 1868. The Senate later held a trial and acquitted him on both counts, allowing him to finish his second term in office.

The scandal dominated the news for months and deeply divided the American public. While Clinton's approval ratings remained relatively strong, the incident damaged his legacy and reshaped public attitudes toward politics and personal conduct.

December 20

Operation Just Cause begins in Panama - 1989

On December 20, 1989, the United States launched Operation Just Cause, a military invasion of Panama aimed at removing dictator Manuel Noriega from power. Noriega had been indicted in the U.S. on drug trafficking charges and was accused of suppressing democracy in Panama.

Over 27,000 U.S. troops participated in the operation. The invasion quickly overpowered Panamanian forces, and Noriega eventually surrendered in early January 1990 after seeking refuge in the Vatican embassy.

The action was criticized by some for civilian casualties and questions of legality, but it succeeded in capturing Noriega and restoring a pro-American government.

The invasion marked one of the largest U.S. military actions between Vietnam and the Gulf War.

December 21

Lockerbie bombing kills 270 - 1988

On December 21, 1988, Pan Am Flight 103 exploded over Lockerbie, Scotland, after a bomb detonated in the cargo hold. All 259 people on board and 11 on the ground were killed.

The flight was en route from London to New York when the attack occurred. Investigators later determined that Libyan agents had planted the explosive device. The bombing became one of the deadliest terrorist acts involving an aircraft at the time.

Years of legal and diplomatic battles followed. Eventually, a Libyan intelligence officer was convicted, and the Libyan government formally accepted responsibility and paid compensation.

The attack led to major changes in airline security and international anti-terrorism efforts.

December 22

Berlin's Brandenburg Gate reopens - 1989

On December 22, 1989, the Brandenburg Gate in Berlin was officially reopened after being closed for nearly three decades. The event symbolized the end of the Cold War and the coming reunification of East and West Germany.

The gate had stood between East and West Berlin, cut off by the Berlin Wall since 1961. After the wall began to fall in November 1989, thousands of people gathered to celebrate at this historic landmark.

West German Chancellor Helmut Kohl and East German Prime Minister Hans Modrow walked through the gate together in a show of unity.

Its reopening marked a powerful moment of hope, peace, and the collapse of communist rule in Eastern Europe.

December 23

U.S. Federal Reserve is created - 1913

On December 23, 1913, President Woodrow Wilson signed the Federal Reserve Act, creating the central banking system of the United States. The Federal Reserve was established to stabilize the financial system and prevent future banking crises.

Before its creation, the U.S. economy suffered from frequent panics and a lack of centralized monetary control. The Fed was given power to regulate banks, manage the money supply, and set interest rates.

It has since become one of the most powerful financial institutions in the world, influencing both domestic and global economies.

The Federal Reserve continues to play a key role in managing inflation, employment, and economic growth.

December 24

Apollo 8 orbits the Moon - 1968

On December 24, 1968, Apollo 8 became the first manned spacecraft to orbit the Moon. Astronauts Frank Borman, Jim Lovell, and William Anders completed ten orbits and returned safely to Earth.

During the mission, the crew read from the Book of Genesis in a Christmas Eve broadcast watched by millions. The iconic "Earthrise" photograph, showing Earth above the lunar horizon, was taken during this mission and became one of the most famous images in history.

Apollo 8 was a critical step in the space race and paved the way for the first Moon landing in 1969.

It remains a symbol of exploration, achievement, and humanity's place in the universe.

December 25

Charlemagne is crowned Emperor - 800

On December 25, 800, Charlemagne was crowned Emperor of the Romans by Pope Leo III in St. Peter's Basilica in Rome. The ceremony revived the idea of a Western Roman Empire and laid the foundation for the Holy Roman Empire.

Charlemagne had expanded the Frankish kingdom across much of Western Europe and promoted education, legal reform, and Christian unity. His coronation gave religious legitimacy to his rule and strengthened ties between the Church and the state.

This moment marked a turning point in medieval Europe, shaping centuries of political and religious history.

Charlemagne is still remembered as one of the most influential rulers of the Middle Ages.

December 26

Tsunami devastates Southeast Asia - 2004

On December 26, 2004, a massive undersea earthquake off the coast of Sumatra triggered a tsunami that struck countries around the Indian Ocean. Waves over 100 feet high killed more than 230,000 people in 14 nations.

It was one of the deadliest natural disasters in recorded history. Indonesia, Sri Lanka, India, and Thailand suffered the most damage. Entire communities were wiped out, and millions were left homeless.

The disaster prompted an unprecedented international relief effort and led to the development of better early warning systems for future tsunamis.

Its global impact united people in grief and humanitarian response.

December 27

Benazir Bhutto is assassinated - 2007

On December 27, 2007, Pakistani opposition leader and former Prime Minister Benazir Bhutto was assassinated at a political rally in Rawalpindi. A gunman shot her, and a suicide bomb exploded shortly afterward.

Bhutto was the first woman to lead a Muslim-majority country and a central figure in Pakistan's political life. Her return from exile had raised hopes for democratic reform, but she faced numerous threats.

Her death plunged Pakistan into turmoil and raised global concern about terrorism and political instability in the region.

Bhutto's legacy as a trailblazer for women and democracy remains significant.

December 28

Nicolae Ceaușescu is executed - 1989

On December 28, 1989, Romanian dictator Nicolae Ceaușescu and his wife, Elena, were executed by firing squad after a swift trial. The execution followed a violent uprising that ended decades of communist rule in Romania.

Ceaușescu's regime was marked by severe repression, economic mismanagement, and a cult of personality. In December 1989, protests escalated into a full revolution. The army turned against him, and he was captured while trying to flee.

His fall was one of the last in a series of Eastern Bloc collapses that year, as communism unravelled across Europe.

His execution marked the dramatic end of one of the harshest regimes in the Soviet sphere.

December 29

Wounded Knee Massacre occurs - 1890

On December 29, 1890, U.S. troops killed nearly 300 Lakota Sioux at Wounded Knee Creek in South Dakota. The massacre followed rising tensions between Native Americans and the government over land, culture, and the Ghost Dance movement.

Soldiers of the 7th Cavalry attempted to disarm a Lakota group when a shot was fired. Chaos followed, and the troops opened fire, including with Hotchkiss guns. Most of the victims were unarmed men, women, and children.

Wounded Knee marked the end of the Indian Wars and symbolized decades of broken treaties and violence.

It remains a tragic and powerful chapter in Native American history.

December 30

Saddam Hussein is executed - 2006

On December 30, 2006, former Iraqi President Saddam Hussein was executed by hanging after being convicted of crimes against humanity. His death followed a controversial trial held after his capture by U.S. forces in 2003.

Saddam had ruled Iraq for over two decades with brutal authority, launching wars against Iran and Kuwait and using chemical weapons against civilians.

His removal and execution were part of the larger Iraq War, but the aftermath left the country unstable and divided. The execution drew mixed reactions and was criticized by some for its conduct and timing.

It marked the end of a brutal dictatorship but opened a new era of uncertainty for Iraq.

December 31

Roman Emperor Commodus is assassinated - 192

On December 31, 192, Roman Emperor Commodus was murdered in his bath, ending a reign marked by instability and excess. Earlier that same day, his mistress Marcia had tried to poison him, but he vomited the poison and survived.

Determined to finish the job, the conspirators enlisted a wrestler named Narcissus, who strangled Commodus while he bathed. The assassination was backed by senators and military officials who feared the emperor's erratic behaviour and growing paranoia.

Commodus had declared himself the reincarnation of Hercules and renamed months after himself. His obsession with gladiatorial combat and disregard for governance had thrown the empire into turmoil.

His death marked the end of the Nerva–Antonine dynasty and ushered in a year of civil war. It also highlighted how absolute power, unchecked, can bring even the mightiest rulers to a brutal end.

Thank You for Reading

Thank you for joining me on this journey through time in ***This Day, That History: 365 Shocking, Strange, and Significant Stories from the Past***. I hope these stories entertained, surprised, and inspired you to dig deeper into the endlessly fascinating world of history.

This is just the beginning as Volume 2 is on the way, filled with even more moments that shaped our world in unexpected and unforgettable ways. Dare I say further volumes down the line…

If you enjoyed this book, I'd greatly appreciate it if you left a review on Amazon. Your support helps keep history alive for more readers to discover (and gives me more motivation to create more books of course!)

Until next time,

Alex Dupont

Printed in Great Britain
by Amazon